# GAINESVILLE
# PUNK

# GAINESVILLE
# PUNK

## A HISTORY OF BANDS & MUSIC

### MATT WALKER

THE
History
PRESS

Published by The History Press
Charleston, SC
www.historypress.net

*Front cover, clockwise from upper left: courtesy of Less Than Jake; photograph by Lindsay Beaumont; photograph by Bryan Wynacht; photograph by Matt Geiger; courtesy of Less Than Jake; courtesy of No Idea Records; photograph by Bryan Wynacht.*
*Back cover: photograph by Tim Hill; top insert: courtesy of No Idea Records; middle insert: courtesy of Matt Sweeting; bottom insert: photograph by Hudson Luce.*

First published 2016

Manufactured in the United States

ISBN 978.1.62619.767.1

Library of Congress Control Number: 2016943510

*To Grace and Cameron*

# CONTENTS

# CONTENTS

# FOREWORD

I went to my first punk show in Gainesville in 1981. The Irritations opened for John Cale. I was eleven years old. The most recent show I caught in Gainesville was probably a few days ago. Always underground, independent, punk.

I don't like big concerts very much. I get off on shows in overlooked spaces: warehouses, people's living rooms, VFW halls, community centers, art galleries, dive bars. I like music made by people with motivations other than making a buck; music with the kind of aggression, political content, social commentary, anger, strangeness and wit that makes it difficult to market. (This doesn't make me better than anyone. It's just what I like.)

As a result, I've been involved with Gainesville's punk scene for more than thirty-five years. And I'm qualified to tell you, the story of Gainesville punk is a mess. Like the music, the story of our scene is dynamic, contradictory, fractious, maybe a little frustrating to understand, possibly overwhelming in large doses.

I love what Matt Walker achieves with this book. He untangles a good portion of this mess, teases out the major threads, hews to what's relevant. He tells the story of Gainesville punk in a clear, direct way that mirrors something else I like about punk: it cuts through the bullshit and gets to the point.

And the story Matt tells here is worth knowing. Gainesville's scene has always been different. Smarter, weirder, a little less violent, a lot more sarcastic. Gainesville bands rep uncool influences. Gainesville's a sleepy southern college town, built on a swamp. The heat and humidity slow us down. The easy living gives us time to mull things over. Gainesville's scene has always put a unique spin on national and regional trends or just sidestepped them altogether. Gainesville incubates. Ideas develop and stew and sometimes emerge to no small effect, rippling out to change the way people all over the world listen to and make music.

*Gainesville Punk: A History of Bands & Music* is going to serve a lot of purposes. It'll give fans insight into the origins and development of their favorite acts. Music history buffs will value the detail it brings to an interesting piece of our broader cultural puzzle. Scene participants from different eras will get context from it, be able to place their time and contributions in a continuum. It'll spur people to seek out and enjoy undervalued music. For some, it'll just be a plain good read. For others, it'll be a way to understand their legacy, an artistic tradition they inherit.

It's this last group that interests me most. My sincere hope is that someone reading this book gets fed up by it and decides to smash that legacy. That someone rebukes this inheritance in a way that surprises and excites us. Gainesville's punk scene has produced a lot of very cool things up to this point, and this book is proof. Now show me what's next.

PATRICK HUGHES

Patrick Hughes wrote the essay collection *Diary of Indignities* for Dark Horse Comics imprint M Press and covered music for *Thrasher*, *JAZZIZ*, *Art Papers* and most Gainesville publications of note. His music writing was first published in *No Idea #3*.

# PREFACE

Thank you for reading this book. When The History Press approached me about the prospect of writing a history of the Gainesville punk scene, I was terrified and excited. I played it cool and gave it some serious consideration for about five seconds before I realized there was no way I could say no. I've been fascinated by the sprawling, intertwining and prolific Gainesville punk scene for years, first as a fan observing it from my hometown in Georgia and then as an enthusiastic participant once I moved to Gainesville a decade ago. To be able to tackle such a huge task is daunting, humbling and ultimately a great privilege. And if you're reading this book, you probably already know that Gainesville's punk music scene has a long and rich history stretching back for decades. This book is not meant to be a complete, encyclopedic recounting of every detail of the scene's history. I have approached this book in a way that I hope provides a solid overview of the scene, a look at some of its important developments and how it got to where it is today. To my knowledge, this is the first book written specifically on this topic. I think it would be great if it can be a jumping-off point for other books to be written that zero in on specific eras or bands mentioned here—to really get into the details. (Jon Resh of Spoke did this with his excellent memoir, *Amped*.)

I don't go into much detail here about the origins or history of punk rock outside of Gainesville—there are tons of great books that have already covered that ground. I also don't spend much time debating the definition of punk or what does or does not qualify a band to be punk. It's a vast genre, and the bands I tend to focus on here exist somewhere along the continuum.

# PREFACE

No matter what they sound like, they generally took a DIY approach to their music and were pushing back against *something*, whether it was social norms, political ideals or just FM rock.

By the way, there are amazing Gainesville punk bands that are not mentioned in this book. Taking on a project like this involves shaping the story into a readable narrative and making some difficult editorial choices. There are places in the book where I could have chosen to highlight a number of different bands, but I ultimately had to choose the ones I thought fit best into *this* narrative. But pay attention to all the Gainesville punk bands named here, and seek them out if you've never heard them. This town has a lot to offer.

# ACKNOWLEDGEMENTS

Thanks to the many, many Gainesville musicians and music fans who helped to make this book possible. People not only went out of their way to sit down for long interviews or multiple email correspondences but also let me rifle through their personal archives of photos, articles and music and answered many annoying one-question emails or text messages from me. And special thanks to my friends and family for providing valuable feedback, support, guidance or advice along the way: my wife, Grace; my mother, Elsie Walker (who passed away before seeing this book completed but who, I can tell you all, was very excited about it); Kenan Davis; Deepak and Susan Kumar; Jason Fernandez; Amy Feldman; P.J. Fancher; Matt Farrell; Jon Reinertsen; Dave Drobach; and JC Kirwan, to name just a few. A big thanks to Patrick Hughes for contributing the foreword and giving me tons of valuable feedback. And thanks go to the photographers who documented the Gainesville scene thanklessly and shared their photos with me to use in this book. Others who provided crucial resources or assistance along the way include Var Thelin, Matt Sweeting, Don Undeen, Brian Alan Ellis, Michael Holt, Marty Williams, Deb Fetzer, Brian Kruger, Marty Jourard (whose book *Music Everywhere* about the 1960s and '70s Gainesville rock scene also came out in 2016) and my crack proofreading team. The full list of interviewees is in the bibliography, but know that each person provided a valuable piece of the big, crazy puzzle that makes up the Gainesville punk scene. I am grateful to you all.

# PART I

# JUST HANGING OUT, 1981–1988

# 1.

# ROACH MOTEL AND GAINESVILLE PUNK'S FIRST WAVE

It was the spring of 1981, and the University of Florida campus in Gainesville was alive with activity as the brief Florida winter quickly faded away and the near-perennial humidity began to seep into the crisp breeze. The bulletin boards that dotted the evergreen campus were covered with flyers advertising shows by southern rock and college cover bands, as were the light poles lining the downtown streets just a short walk east on University Avenue. One flyer stood out among the Skynyrd wannabes and Beatles believers. It displayed a cut-out drawing of a human fetus with a coat hanger through its head, adjacent to an image showing another fetus floating in a bowl of cereal. This wasn't yet another group of college kids rehashing 1970s radio rock. This was different, subversive, interesting. It was punk rock.

The bombastic flyer was advertising the very first show for a new band called Roach Motel. Even the letters used to spell out the band's name on the flyer—each one cut out in jagged, ransom-note fashion—announced that this was not your normal Gainesville band.

The flyer, despite the small college town's liberal leanings, was over the line for some in the community. Protests began forming across the street from Friday Night Live, the tiny new wave dance club where the show was scheduled, spearheaded by the burgeoning religious right organization the Moral Majority—a national group led by evangelist preacher Jerry Falwell. It wasn't long before the *Gainesville Sun* newspaper got wind of the protests and the local television crews began showing up. The owner of Friday Night

A flyer for what would have been the first Roach Motel show. The show was cancelled after the flyer drew controversy from the community. *Courtesy of Jeff Hodapp.*

Live, under pressure from the vocal minority and threat of eviction from the landlord, decided to cancel the show.

The young punks in Roach Motel laughed it off, just as they laughed most everything off. But founding member and guitarist George Tabb says that, although he may have been laughing along outwardly with his bandmates, he was secretly devastated. He had been brimming with excitement to play his first punk rock show, and the cancellation was a serious blow.


George Tabb moved to Gainesville to attend the University of Florida in January 1980. He grew up in Greenwich, Connecticut, the child of a divorced family with a harsh, abusive father and a mother and stepfather who encouraged his artistic side. Tabb had been forced to move to Florida for his high school years when his father relocated to a farm near Tallahassee, the state capital. Tabb hated living in Florida and with his father, and he relished his trips back to the Northeast to visit his mother. It was on one of these trips that Tabb's path was laid out before him—galvanized into existence by the three-chord attack of a band called The Ramones. His mother and stepfather had taken him to see the genre-defining punks at New York's legendary CBGB club, and Tabb's life was never the same.

When Tabb finished high school in Tallahassee, he jumped at the chance to move two and a half hours southeast to Gainesville and the University of Florida and out from under the heavy hand of his father. Gainesville opened up a whole new world for Tabb; he even got to see his beloved Ramones again when they played at the Florida Gym at UF in March of that year.

That summer, Tabb got his first guitar during a trip to New York and soon learned how to bang out a few basic power chords. Back in Gainesville, he met another UF student named Paul Miller. Despite Tabb's Jewish heritage and Miller's proclivities for Nazi garb and memorabilia, they bonded over their love of punk rock. Tabb remembers sitting in Miller's apartment and hearing Black Flag's *Jealous Again* EP for the first time. Miller also happened to play bass. The obvious next step was to form their very own punk band. They just needed a singer and a drummer.

Like Tabb, Bob Fetz had moved to Gainesville to attend UF. He had arrived in 1979, but by the time he met Tabb and Miller (introduced by a mutual friend, Eric Engan, from the local punk/new wave cover band The Bazookas), he had dropped out of school and was working as an Electrolux vacuum cleaner salesman. Fetz grew up in New Jersey and, like Tabb, was fully inducted into the world of punk rock by the time he hit Gainesville. From his high school days, he was close friends with members of punk legends The Misfits and other active New Jersey bands.

Also like Tabb, Fetz sought an outlet and conduit to the punk rock world while in Gainesville, which was so far away from CBGB's that it might as well have existed in another galaxy. Focusing his desires and using his punk rock connections from back home, Fetz started a magazine called *Destroy*, a cut-and-paste DIY fanzine that featured interviews and album reviews—and dripped with satire and dark humor.

To the surprise of his friend Engan, Fetz told Tabb and Miller that he was a singer; the three quickly arranged a practice. Fetz arrived at Miller's apartment with an Electrolux in hand—as good a time as any for a sales pitch. After an unsuccessful vacuum demo, which ended with an ashtray full of cigarette butts on the carpet, Tabb, Fetz and Miller started jamming on some rough song ideas Tabb had been working on. With no drummer, Tabb and Miller plunked away at the rudimentary sketches of songs while Fetz proceeded to growl, scream, thrash and roll around on the filthy floor. It was a perfect match.

From the beginning, Roach Motel was never going to be a typical Gainesville band—punk or otherwise. One major difference that set it apart was the fact that, besides a couple of early staples in their live set, the members weren't learning cover songs. Roach Motel wrote their own songs—a novel idea in Gainesville at the time. Looking back, it's no big surprise, considering the punk rock and hardcore movement from which they sprang. But Tabb says it was also partially by default.

"The truth of the matter was I could not learn other songs, could not figure them out," Tabb says. "I learned [the Dead Boys' song] 'Sonic Reducer' from Eric…so we would play 'Sonic Reducer' and [The Ramones' song] 'Blitzkrieg Bop' in the set along with all the originals. I wanted to do Ramones songs, but I couldn't figure them out, so we were an original band."

In those early months, Tabb, Miller and Fetz devoted their time to practicing and writing songs, sometimes with a drummer, sometimes without. Their doomed Friday Night Live debut came and went. A few months later, they got on a show with Engan's band The Bazookas at Catch-22, an occasional venue for locals that Tabb recalls being a redneck club, "way the fuck out in the sticks."

Gainesville had long been a music town, nurturing the early careers of Tom Petty; Stephen Stills of Crosby, Stills and Nash; and Don Felder and Bernie Leadon of The Eagles. But the town's rock clubs had taken a hit in the late 1970s with the rise of disco. The clubs that remained were dominated by those Skynyrd knockoffs, Top 40 cover bands, hard-rock rehashers and country acts. Despite balking at the first hint of controversy at Roach Motel's failed premiere, Friday Night Live was the first venue in town to promote itself as catering to a punk and new wave crowd. Reality Kitchen, a hippie-ish café and art space downtown, also hosted punk acts occasionally, less because of a solidarity with the punk ethos than to support local art and music. The far-flung Catch-22 and Hogsbreath Saloon also served as occasional punk venues, even if it was not their primary crowd.

From time to time, other venues would decide to have a "punk night" or a "new wave night" after reading about the latest music trends. But after attracting crowds of rowdy, cheap, ripped-clothes-wearing, parking-lot-drinking punk kids, the "punk night" would quickly disappear from their schedules.

With no consistent clubs offering a home for punk rock, rented recreational spaces like the American Legion Hall and houses in the "student ghetto"—just north and northeast of the UF campus—would play host to the bulk of punk shows for the genre's tiny scene throughout the 1980s.

While Roach Motel embodied most aspects of a true "punk" band, there were a handful of other bands in Gainesville in those days that were working to fill the punk and new wave niche. Among them were Riff Raff (later called The Riff), one of the more popular early punk bands in Gainesville, remembered fondly for their energetic performances of punk covers; The Invasion, another popular cover band, this one leaning toward the new wave end of the spectrum, with some originals coming later that evoked shades of U2 in their prime; and The Irritations, a snotty group that played a mix of covers and originals that eventually tried to eschew their "punk roots" as they aspired to mainstream success. Others like The Atomics or Engan's Bazookas would play popular punk covers at parties.

The University of Florida was a surprisingly strong supporter of left-of-center bands in the late 1970s and early 1980s. In addition to The Ramones show that Tabb saw, The Cramps, The Police and Devo all played UF-hosted gigs in Gainesville during that time. In 1981, The Invasion even opened up for U2 on its first extensive U.S. tour, at The Rathskeller, a UF cafeteria and rec center.

Also in 1981, the annual UF-sponsored Halloween Ball reached its height of reckless debauchery. Beginning years before as an annual concert and hippie-leaning celebration, the Halloween Ball had gradually devolved into an annual bacchanalia on campus. Notorious shock punks The Plasmatics, led by the sexually provocative performance artist Wendy O. Williams, headlined the ball that year. It was quickly evident that UF organizers may have gotten in over their heads, as Williams wielded a chainsaw on stage, sawing at least one guitar in half. A car that sat on the stage turned out to be rigged with explosives; when detonated, it caused a massive blast that was further amplified by the giant concert PA speakers, leaving some in the crowd reeling from the noise. After The Plasmatics, the Halloween Ball would limp along for a few more years in a much more controlled incarnation before quietly disappearing completely.

By the time Roach Motel's debut at Catch-22 was imminent, the band still hadn't procured a regular drummer, so they recruited their friend Dorsey Martin from Tampa hardcore band Rat Cafeteria to fill in. They had one practice with Martin on the day of the show. Since Martin didn't know the songs, Tabb would lift the neck of his guitar up and drop it back down to signal the end of a song.

That night, Roach Motel took the stage for the first time with the perfect combination of attitude, confidence and cluelessness. Tabb sported a self-described "Jew-fro" atop eyes blackened with eyeliner, while Miller stood shirtless with the words "Zyklon B" painted across his chest. Martin sat behind the drums, poised to play along to a bunch of songs he had heard only once. And Fetz offered a thin, wiry figure whose slight appearance would only make his explosive energy and presence all the more striking and sometimes even scary for onlookers. They set their sights on the status quo.

As they ripped into their first song, Fetz unleashed his growling, rolling, drunken screaming frontman routine on the tiny Catch-22 crowd. The performance was sloppy, rudimentary and rude—and unlike anything Gainesville had seen before. It was aggressive, dirty and scary in a way the previous crop of Gainesville punk-influenced bands was not. By the end of the vigorous debut, Fetz—a severe diabetic—was suffering from a combination of low blood sugar, excessive booze and exhaustion. Tabb had to drive him to the hospital in what would become a semi-regular routine following Roach Motel shows.

In the coming months, Roach Motel would play out in Gainesville whenever they could, honing their furious amalgamation of punk and hardcore. Although the band held fast to the barely controlled chaos and energy of their live shows, they progressively grew more cohesive, though they would never be palatable for a mainstream crowd. But that was the point.

Like its music, Roach Motel was a volatile band. Tabb's and Fetz's strong personalities would frequently clash, resulting in ongoing bouts of antagonizing and constant one-upping contests. Miller quickly exited the group, replaced for a time by bassist Rhonda Glissendorf, who was eventually replaced by Eric Engan, who would be Roach Motel's longest-running bass player. Tabb and Fetz remained the most constant members as they cycled through drummers, including a sixteen-year-old named Chad Salter, who would go on to play in many Gainesville bands over the years and was one of the early guitarists for legendary metal band Neurosis.

Despite the rotating cast of bassists and drummers, Roach Motel continued gathering steam, playing shows in Gainesville and around Florida whenever they got a chance. Other punk and hardcore bands started to spring up around them. Gainesville local John McGuigan (whom Tabb credits as being a kind of punk rock mentor for him at the time) formed a hardcore band called Liquid Plumbers, which also included Engan and a guitarist from Fort Lauderdale named Jeff Hodapp.

In the small world of early '80s hardcore punk, Roach Motel quickly began attracting attention in pockets across the country. Like Minor Threat in Washington, D.C., or Black Flag in Los Angeles, Roach Motel were venturing into uncharted territory, illuminated by a Ramones-loving guitar player with a three-chord repertoire and an acerbic, nihilistic prankster armed with a microphone. If there had been a rulebook for Gainesville bands at the time, Roach Motel doused it in kerosene, set it on fire and kicked it into the audience.

During this time, Fetz was particularly industrious at networking with other bands in the underground punk scene through his early punk connections and *Destroy* magazine. So, when Black Flag planned a short Florida tour in May 1982, Roach Motel was tapped as the opener.

In the book *American Hardcore: A Tribal History*, Tabb recalls meeting up with the most notorious L.A. hardcore band of the day: "Black Flag shows up at my Gainesville apartment; it's all these guys that look like hippies. I'm like, 'Who the fuck are these longhairs?'" Tabb goes on to say that the longhairs got him kicked out of his apartment after the band jumped into his complex's pool fully clothed.

The two bands hit the road, playing in Fort Lauderdale, Tampa and Daytona. The irony of the lineup of Black Flag/Roach Motel—both named after pest control products—was not lost on the band members. The shows on that short tour were extremely violent affairs, as hardcore shows often were. A member of the Tampa crowd had his jaw broken in three places, and Fetz was dragged off the stage by his feet—"his head going bump-

bump-bump down the steps," like in a cartoon, notes an article from the *Independent Florida Alligator*, UF's unofficial student newspaper.

Liquid Plumbers guitarist Jeff Hodapp had tagged along on the Florida tour, and when Roach Motel got home, they asked him to join the band as the lead guitarist. Hodapp happily agreed—they were one of his favorite bands after all—and within a week the band was in a Gainesville recording studio preparing for their first release.

The recording session turned out to be a disaster. The band suffered through the engineer—obviously ignorant of punk rock and hardcore—deriding their talents and songwriting skills. In the end, the quality of the recording was so poor the band could only keep two of the five songs they recorded. Next, Roach Motel booked time with the more reputable Bob McPeek at Mirror Image Studios. By this time, Frank Mullen had joined the band and would stick as Roach Motel's most long-running drummer.

In the fall of 1982, Roach Motel released the six-song seven-inch *Roach & Roll* on their own label, Destroy Records. It was the first vinyl release by a Gainesville punk band—recorded, designed, packaged and released on the band's own terms without the help of any big names or established record labels. The feat was virtually unheard of in Gainesville. For the release, six hundred records were pressed. Today, the seven-inch record is considered a collectible, selling for up to seventy-five dollars per copy.

*Roach & Roll*'s track listing included two songs from Roach Motel's first recording session, "I Hate the Sunshine State" and "Now You're Gonna Die," and four songs from the Mirror Image session, "Shut Up," "Creep," "More Beer" and the problematic "Wetback."

"Wetback" was a song written by a member of one of Hodapp's earlier bands about the rising Mexican population in Texas. Although it was meant as an over-the-top, tongue-in-cheek affair—their songs didn't typically tackle political or social issues in any serious manner—the band subsequently omitted it from later compilations and anthologies and readily acknowledge that it may have been a misguided venture to record the song in the first place.

On the other hand, "More Beer," with its repetitive, triumphant anthem of, yes, "More beer!" is perhaps Gainesville's first punk anthem. It was a sentiment the punks could get behind, and the song was catchy, to boot.

Later that year, Roach Motel organized the city's first punk rock festival, Florida Slamfest '82, at the Star Garage in downtown Gainesville. Roach Motel headlined the eight-band fest, with other locals Terminal Fun and Slime and out-of-towners like Rat Cafeteria and the Sluts, from New

Roach Motel's 1982 EP, *Roach & Roll*, the first vinyl record by a Gainesville punk band. *Courtesy of Jeff Hodapp.*

Orleans, helping to fill out the bill. A sign leading into the venue read, "Not responsible for injury or death."

Roach Motel continued to gain notoriety in the underground punk and hardcore scenes of the day; the problem was that they did not fit nicely into either category. The band's fast, aggressive, chaotic music and live performances, combined with their DIY ethics, put them in the hardcore category with the Minor Threats and the Black Flags of the day. But they had the nihilistic, don't-give-a-fuck attitude of first wave punk acts like the Sex Pistols (and in many ways were even more sincerely snotty than their English predecessors), evidenced by Fetz's drunken performances, in which he maintained little to no regard for his own or others' well-being.

Perhaps the most notable attribute of Roach Motel besides their music was their sense of humor, which carried through to nearly everything they did. They didn't take much of anything seriously, constantly making jabs at punk rock, hardcore, other bands, each other and even their fans. "Our audience is really scum sometimes," Hodapp said in an *Alligator* article.

But they were serious about being a band, driven by the thrill and passion of it all, if not by technical prowess. A band that's not serious about what they're doing doesn't spend endless hours and energy booking and playing shows, creating and distributing a magazine and recording and self-releasing music.

Tom Nordlie, a Gainesville musician and music journalist from the mid-1980s through early '90s, notes that, from the beginning, Roach Motel didn't seek to be legitimized by anybody. "They didn't aspire to the big time, they acted as though annoying people around Gainesville *was* the big time," Nordlie says. "Here in this little fish pond they changed the game, permanently. They were legit because they carried on as though they were legit, and they dared the rest of the world to prove otherwise. Nobody stepped up to take their challenge."

The punk and hardcore scenes were growing in Florida, along with Roach Motel's popularity. In March 1983, Minor Threat made their way to Gainesville, playing the American Legion Hall with Roach Motel, Hated Youth, Sector 4 and Moral Sex. The hardcore pioneers crashed with Fetz and his girlfriend Cindy Frey—for a week. When Minor Threat played a show in Orlando, they even drove back to Gainesville that same night to stay in Fetz's trailer.

Roach Motel's connection with the D.C. hardcore band would come in handy later, when a Baltimore show was cancelled. The band left the venue with no place to play and nowhere to sleep. Minor Threat stepped in and helped Roach Motel weasel their way onto a Suicidal Tendencies show. Afterward, the members of Roach Motel crashed at the now-fabled Dischord House, the birthplace of the legendary D.C.-based record label.

Later in 1983, Roach Motel put out what would become one of Florida's most influential early hardcore records on their Destroy label—a compilation of Florida hardcore bands called *We Can't Help It If We're from Florida*. The seven-inch record featured songs from Hated Youth, Sector 4, Morbid Opera and Rat Cafeteria. It also debuted three new Roach Motel songs, including "My Dog's into Anarchy." The seven-inch is revered as a shining and influential snapshot of early Florida hardcore. Its influence carries through to today, in part because it happened to fall into the hands of

A flyer advertising a show featuring hardcore pioneers Minor Threat, with Gainesville's Roach Motel and Moral Sex and Tallahassee's Hated Youth and Sector 4. *Courtesy of Jeff Hodapp.*

a young Gainesville teenager who would help bring Gainesville's punk scene to a broader audience across the country.

By the end of the year, Roach Motel shows were becoming increasingly violent, beyond even what the band was comfortable with. The hardcore scene was growing; where Roach Motel had combined their love of The Ramones and the Dead Boys and mixed it up with contemporaries like Minor Threat, the younger kids coming into the scene had started out with hardcore, not understanding the subtleties of its short history. They were there strictly for the aggression.

Tensions were also rising within Roach Motel. By this time, Russ Avery, who also sang for Gainesville garage punks Slime, was handling bass duties. Tabb and Fetz's relationship was as volatile as ever, and Tabb had his own friction with Avery.

The band landed a gig in Tampa opening for the Dead Kennedys at the Cuban Club. The maximum-capacity crowd was the biggest audience Roach Motel had ever played to. And it would be Tabb's final show as a member of the band. The show was chaos from start to finish.

A member of a band that Roach Motel had an earlier tiff with tried to assault Tabb with a knife in the middle of a song before being pushed back into the audience, and at one point Fetz disappeared into the crowd, only to

Roach Motel performs at the Cuban Club in Tampa, opening for the Dead Kennedys.
*Courtesy of Jeff Hodapp.*

be thrown back onstage with no shoes and no microphone. He was then hit by his shoe as it was flung through the air on its return mission. And, at the end of it all, Roach Motel had to pay for the lost microphone.

After that night, Tabb decided he wanted to separate himself from the violence and what he saw as a scene moving in a hateful and dangerous direction. He continued on with his sporadic solo act, The George Tabb Experience, and later the "peace-punk" band Atoms for Peace.

# 2.

# GAINESVILLE PUNK'S
# NEW TORCHBEARERS

In the early 1980s, Roach Motel positioned themselves as the essential Gainesville (and Florida) punk band. They were the clear frontrunners of a young, very small scene in Gainesville. Although bands came and went in those early years, nobody truly challenged Roach Motel as city punk rock champions. But one band stepped up to carry their torch: the Mutley Chix.

Formed by a group of young women who had landed in Gainesville from various places around the same time as Roach Motel, the Mutley Chix would put their own spin on the male-dominated hardcore of the day and eventually become the de facto gatekeepers of the tiny Gainesville scene.

Guitarist Debra Fetzer remembers seeing Roach Motel for the first time after John McGuigan of Terminal Fun and Liquid Plumbers gave her a flyer for a show. The experience formed a lifelong connection to punk rock. "It just totally changed my life, literally, because it was just like, whoa—this is a *band* and I can do that. Like *I* can do that," Fetzer says.

The original Mutley Chix lineup of Fetzer on guitar, Lois Sakany on vocals, Sharon Lassen on drums and Cindy Frey on bass were coaxed into playing their first show during a house party at Sakany's in August 1984. (Fetzer notes that because Frey was also Bob Fetz's girlfriend, she helped give the group "cred" points at the time.) The women had been talking up their new punk band to their friends and fellow punk fans for weeks if not months, but nobody had seen any evidence of it. Finally, some of the partygoers were fed up of hearing the group talk about it and just handed them instruments. Reluctant, scared and excited, they played the show. The Mutley Chix acknowledge that it might not have been a shining debut, but they stepped up when it was called for. A new chapter in Gainesville punk was opened.

Like Roach Motel, Mutley Chix were an industrious band in their first few years. Sakany began her own punk hardcore fanzine, *No Worries*, which all of the members of Chix contributed to in some form. Along with John McGuigan, Sakany also led the way in booking punk shows in Gainesville. Even a 1985 *Alligator* article notes Sakany's industriousness in booking national underground acts. Among the groups booked under Sakany's watch were Agnostic Front, Sonic Youth and Scream. And Mutley Chix, having usually organized the show, had first choice of which shows they wanted to play.

By the mid-'80s, Gainesville was still lacking a steady venue for underground music, so the Chix would often book a touring band and then rent out a room like the American Legion Hall or a community rec center. They also had to come up with a PA system, which was usually supplied by their friends and fellow musicians Greg Ceton and Michael Murphy. Ceton and Murphy would also become Gainesville's unofficial music documentarians of the day, as they would often record punk shows. They even recorded some "official" releases by early Gainesville punk bands on their four-track recorder. (Photographer Hudson Luce was usually on hand to document the visual side of things in those days.)

By all accounts—including their own—Mutley Chix weren't very good when they started playing. They were all passion and little skill, basically learning their instruments in public—not an uncommon position to be in for a young punk band in a small town. That would change over time, but the passion of their live performances was enough to get the attention of the Gainesville punk scene. By mid-1985, the *Alligator* said the group had "a small but loyal cultish following."

Sakany says:

> *I don't think we thought that we were part of something that mattered significantly. We were just following what we thought was fun and made sense. I think one of the backdrops that we did play against was the story of uber University of Florida nationalism....On campus, you had this conservative sorority, fraternity, business school mentality....We probably came from a long line of people who were repelled by that lock-step behavior and thought there was something a little bit wrong with it.*

Original Mutley Chix member and second lead singer Sharon Lassen flies through the air at a house show while Cindy Frey plays bass. *Photograph by Hudson Luce.*

The Mutley Chix's music was fueled by the same rebellious energy as that of Roach Motel. Songs like "Jack at Bageland" were imbued with just as much hardcore ferocity as any first wave hardcore song ever was. (They even covered Roach Motel's drunken anthem, "More Beer.") But other songs, like the dirge-y "Hangin' Out," took on a more relaxed, spacey quality; like many of those early songs, it evoked a sense of apathetic cool, like a less experimental Sonic Youth. They were the disaffected youth of the 1980s, but they couldn't be bothered too much to care either way.

An early supporter of the Mutley Chix and the Gainesville punk scene in general was a homeless man named Robert Peterson. Peterson would frequently hang out at the student ghetto house shows and after parties and was a fixture in the '80s scene. It was no surprise that Peterson migrated toward the vital young punk scene. He was actually an accomplished piano player and organist who had played in the 1960s rock band The McCoys with a young Rick Derringer, best known for their song "Hang on Sloopy." He was also rumored to have jammed with Jimi Hendrix. Peterson was likely suffering from an undiagnosed mental illness, which led to harder and harder times and, eventually, a life on the street.

One day when Sakany was complaining that their songs were never played on the local radio stations, Peterson was surprised. He told Sakany that the Mutley Chix would surely be on the radio one day. In a sense, he was right. Mutley Chix never became radio sensations, but their overall sound—combining early punk and hardcore, slowing it down a touch and adding a slight ethereal sensibility—didn't sound all that different from the alt-rock that would later dominate the airwaves in the early to mid-1990s.

The Mutley Chix were the revered scene queens of the day for a lot of the punk fans in Gainesville, but, being an all-woman group in the '80s,

A flyer advertising a show with The Flaming Lips and Gainesville's Mutley Chix, Just Demi-Gods and Subject. *Courtesy of Matt Sweeting.*

they also faced more than their share of sexism and intimidation. Some town scenesters wouldn't acknowledge them as a "real band," and their ability to create and perform was questioned, even while surpassing their male peers through their music and their contributions in fostering the local scene. Rather than lashing out against the naysayers, the Chix handled the discrimination by largely ignoring it and continuing to prove their talents at their wild live shows and in their recordings.

"There was less awareness around back then. You just took it. We accepted it and didn't necessarily have the framework to fight against it," Sakany says. "It was just more accepted. Every '-ism' was more accepted back then. You were just like, 'Ok, this is what they want to call us. Whatever.' I didn't care. I didn't give a fuck, really, what people think about me. I never have."

Mutley Chix weren't a "girl punk band"; they were a punk band that happened to have all female members—rocking just as hard as the next group, probably harder.


Just as Mutley Chix were gaining momentum in Gainesville's underground, Roach Motel came to an unceremonious end. The Gainesville punk forefathers had released their second seven-inch, *What the Hell, It's Roach Motel*, in 1984 and were gearing up to finally record their full-length debut the following year. Guitarist Hodapp graduated from UF with a business degree and moved back to South Florida. This was and still is a common challenge Gainesville bands face—since most of the UF students are not actually from Gainesville, it's inevitable that someone will eventually earn a degree (the original reason to move to Gainesville) and move back home. The band knew its days might be numbered, yet there was some hope that the full-length album would create enough momentum to keep things going in some form.

Hodapp had been in charge of the band fund. When he was getting ready to move back to Fort Lauderdale, he left the Roach Motel bank account in the care of bassist Russ Avery, who promptly emptied the account and skipped town, leaving the band flat broke. No money, no album, no fanfare. Roach Motel was finished.

But in the early 2000s, something unexpected happened: each member of Roach Motel received a check in the mail from Avery, totaling the sum of money he took from the band in 1985.

# 3.

# A NEW 'ZINE IN TOWN

**V**ar Thelin was a freshman at Gainesville High School in 1984 when he discovered punk rock. Thelin was intrigued by a small group of older kids in school who would read punk rock 'zines in gym class and trade mysterious cassette tapes in the hallways. But the kids didn't immediately acquiesce to his attempts to be let in to their secret world. In those days, learning about punk rock took effort—writing letters, tracking down 'zines, sending off for a tape in the mail that might arrive a month later and would hopefully have one or two decent songs on it. But Thelin persisted; eventually, one of his classmates loaned him a cassette. One side had Black Flag's *Damaged* on it, and the other side was *We Can't Help It If We're from Florida* and Roach Motel's *What the Hell, It's Roach Motel.*

"I put it on headphones and put the blanket over my head at night and listened to it and was both really freaked out by it and kind of scared, but at the same time incredibly intrigued," Thelin says. "I'm actually pretty proud that that was the thing that got me into hardcore and actual punk was Florida music."

Thelin and his good friend Ken Coffelt began going to local punk shows, often the only high schoolers in a room full of college-age punks or older. In Gainesville, this wasn't usually a problem, because most of the shows were still largely held in rented spaces or at house parties. The Gainesville punk scene was also still small enough that virtually every punk fan in town could fit in a student ghetto living room, so Thelin and Coffelt quickly became familiar to the older regulars.

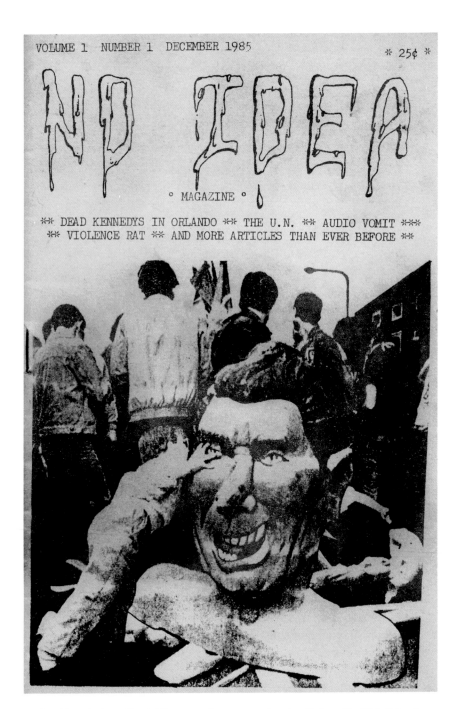

*No Idea Magazine* issue No. 1. The magazines were printed at Gainesville High School. *Courtesy of Ken Coffelt.*

At the time, Coffelt was also making his own handmade comic books called *Rat Comics*. Thelin was impressed that someone he knew could create an actual, real, tangible publication. With their newly discovered world of punk, it wasn't long before Thelin and Coffelt, along with a handful of friends (calling themselves The Droogs), began collecting material and designing the first issue of their very own 'zine. With the help of one of their high school teachers and the printing press at Gainesville High School, the *No Idea* fanzine was born.

It wasn't until after the first issue was out that Thelin realized the name was very close to that of the Mutley Chix 'zine, *No Worries*. Thelin was a little embarrassed once he made the connection, but he quickly settled into the name and liked the fact that it was sort of an allusion to another punk 'zine in town.

*No Idea* No. 1, appearing in December 1985, featured a strange oversized bust of then-president Ronald Reagan adorning the cover. The first page reads: "Think of vermin breeding in rotting flesh. Think of the stench of putrefying pigshit. Think of scumsucking maggots feeding on disease drenched diarrhea. Now think of skating forever on the perfect wooden ramp. Think of beautiful wildflowers. Think of living forever in peace on a clean Earth. See the contrast? That's NO IDEA."

Among the contents of the sixteen-page black-and-white 'zine were a review of a Dead Kennedys show in Orlando; an editorial about the United Nations; several album reviews; a comical review of the popcorn at Gainesville's various movie theaters; ads for local businesses, including Hyde and Zeke's Records and Einstein's Records; and a *Violence Rat* comic.

As the first issue of *No Idea* was rolling off the presses, a new Gainesville band called Psychic Violents would play their first show and push the young Gainesville punk scene into uncharted territory.

# 4.

# PSYCHIC VIOLENTS EXPLORE

Psychic Violents, formed from the remnants of two short-lived local punk bands, quickly became a fixture in the Gainesville scene. Frontman Charles Pinion was in his late twenties and working as an art teacher at a high school in Gainesville when he says he truly discovered punk rock. As an artist, Pinion had always felt that he had his finger on the pulse of the underground, but then he began to notice that the skater kids at the high school were listening to bands like Dead Kennedys and other punk rock he had never heard before. "I still thought Talking Heads were really cool and cutting edge, but by this point they were doing *Stop Making Sense* or whatever," Pinion says.

Pinion would soon leave his teaching job and fully immerse himself in the worlds of art and punk. After his first band, Swamp Medicine, quickly fizzled, Pinion hooked up with the members of another recently disbanded group called Village Virus to form Psychic Violents.

Unlike Roach Motel or Mutley Chix, the members of Psychic Violents were adept at their instruments from the very beginning. Bassist Jorge Cervera was the most inexperienced in the beginning, but after playing for only about eight weeks, he sounded like an accomplished if not innovative bass player. Guitarist Sam Gough was possibly the best guitar player the Gainesville punk scene had witnessed up to that point, with a playing style that could move seamlessly between a Minutemen jangle, lightning-fast technical solos and cutting hardcore power chords. Drummer Dave Dickey had been discovered by Cervera and Gough for Village Virus when they heard him playing in a student ghetto garage. He wasn't even a punk fan, but his drumming had stopped them in their tracks and they banged on the garage door and recruited him right there. As for Pinion, with his art background, he brought an element of theatricality and a strong, often dark, visual aesthetic.

Psychic Violents played their first show in December 1985 at a house party for their friend Ric "Stick" Green. Their second show, shortly after that, was at a newly opened bottle club called The Vatican, located at 6 East University Avenue in downtown Gainesville.

Even though places like Reality Kitchen and Hogsbreath Saloon hosted punk shows from time to time in the early 1980s, The Vatican was the first venue that might be considered a home for punk rock in Gainesville. It was the first club that was owned, booked and operated by fans of punk rock with the goal of supporting local music and booking touring punk bands. The club was opened by a crew of six people, four of whom were UF students. Everyone had their specialized roles, but each of the students would take a semester off from school to focus on managing the venue. The Vatican carried on strong for about two years before it changed ownership. Without the spark of the original crew, it lost its footing and quickly fizzled out.

Psychic Violents stood out in the tiny scene because they took the punk and hardcore that came before them and pushed it into areas previously unexplored in Gainesville punk. Like Roach Motel and Mutley Chix, they brought something new and fresh to the scene. Cervera says they were a hardcore band for about six weeks but quickly tired of playing

A flyer advertising a show featuring Gainesville's Psychic Violents and The Smegmas at The Bar. *Courtesy of Charles Pinion.*

the same stripped-down, simplistic formula. They wanted a challenge. They used hardcore as a base and jumped off into all directions.

For the most part in early hardcore—and for many punk bands—the guitar was squarely locked in with the bass and drums, creating a driving blast of distorted power. Psychic Violents took a more dynamic approach. Where Cervera and Dickey would lock in with the rhythm section, Gough would add a layer above the rhythm, accenting and emphasizing melody and mood.

The Minutemen were a big influence on Gough's guitar playing, and D. Boon's death shortly after Psychic Violents' first show at The Vatican weighed heavily on the band early in their development. They even wrote two separate Minutemen/D. Boon tributes, "Boonesberry" and "Boonesville."

Psychic Violents' live shows were commanding not only because of the intricate musicianship at play but also for Pinion's singular presence as a frontman. Pinion brought his art to the stage. A tall, thin, striking figure, Pinion would become fully immersed in his role as singer/performer during Psychic Violents shows—at times taking the stage in intricate zombie makeup. Slightly menacing and potentially unhinged, Pinion's frontman persona and aesthetic foreshadowed the horror movies he would go on to make in his career.

Psychic Violents perform at The Vatican. *Photograph by Hudson Luce.*

Pinion also took an aggressive approach to creating merchandise and art for Psychic Violents. He designed and printed T-shirts before they even played their first show. Cervera remembers that, within a week of forming, "Charles had flooded the town with this sort of obtuse eyeball artwork that just was on every phone pole everywhere."

Pinion recalls that some in the punk scene thought the T-shirts were premature. He attributes his attitude toward proliferating merch to being slightly older than a lot of the other punks in the scene and, as a "late bloomer," having more of a sense of urgency: "Who gives a shit about it's premature....I could be dead tomorrow."

Pinion took a similar approach to releasing music. The default professional recording studio at the time was still Mirror Image Studios, where Roach Motel had recorded a majority of their songs. But Mirror Image was too expensive for most of the DIY punk bands at the time.

Instead, Psychic Violents made the "Red Tape"—a thirty-minute cassette tape recorded on Pinion's boombox—and sold it at shows for $2.50. Pinion would decorate small cardboard boxes and write "Local Music" on them and take them around to record stores to try to get them to keep it on the counter. He would include the Psychic Violents' tape and encouraged other local bands to add to the box. "I'm not just trying to promote myself, I think we could all have a more vibrant scene if we kind of supported each other," Pinion says. "It seems so basic but it was a big deal to convince these fucking people, including Hyde and Zeke's for God's sake."

If there was a record store that served as a central hub for the Gainesville punk

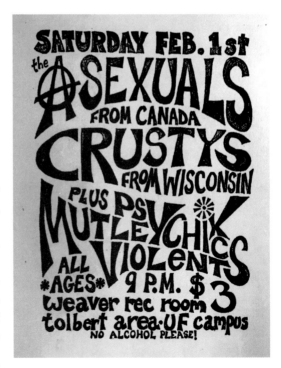

A flyer advertising the first show Mutley Chix and Psychic Violents played together. *Courtesy of Charles Pinion.*

scene in those days, it was Hyde and Zeke's. It had the broadest selection of music in town in the 1980s and a staff that specialized in a wide array of genres. It had something for everyone, including the punks. Mirror Image's Bob McPeek was the original co-owner of Hyde and Zeke Records, along with Ric Kaestner. They opened the doors in 1977 and sold the store to new owners in 1986. It flailed for a few years before thriving again after it was purchased in 1990 by Charlie Scales, one of Hyde and Zeke's earliest employees. The store eventually closed in 2013 after Scales passed away.

The second issue of *No Idea* came out in March 1986 and featured an interview with Gainesville's newest wave-making punks, Psychic Violents. In the interview, Thelin asks the very broad question, "Are you pleased with your sound?" perhaps hinting at how Psychic Violents' music didn't quite fit neatly into the punk or hardcore mold. Cervera's answer, even then, showed a desire to shed labels: "I think that from my standpoint that we're trying to be really melodic, while still having punch. You have so many hardcore bands that just sound really aggressive and real thick and real mean. It doesn't make it very accessible to all the people, when you hear this guitar charging at you."

The thirty-six-page *No Idea* No. 2 also included an April show schedule for The Vatican and a call for bands seeking to play in Gainesville to either contact The Droogs at *No Idea* or The Vatican directly. By this time, Thelin had begun Weasel Productions and, with a little guidance and blessings from Sakany and the Chix, had begun booking punk shows in town.

Meanwhile, the Mutley Chix were still going strong. But the band would soon make some lineup changes—a trend that would carry on for the rest of their existence. Sharon Lassen was going to Alaska for the summer and wasn't sure if she would be coming back to Gainesville. As a replacement, they got one of their good friends, Deborah Phillips, aka English (previously of Swamp Medicine), to play drums in Lassen's place. Singer Lois Sakany was also nearing graduation from UF and would be moving on from Gainesville in the not-too-distant future.

The original members and the new incarnation of the Chix got together with Greg Ceton and Michael Murphy to record their first tape before Lassen took off to Alaska. The self-titled, self-released album includes the original lineup of Sakany on vocals, Beatty on drums, Frey on bass and Fetzer on guitar, as well as songs with the newest member, English, on drums and Lassen switching over to lead vocals. They wanted to document their earliest lineup and provide a segue to the new Chix. Though Lassen took over lead vocal duties during that time, eventually all the Mutley Chix would sing and even trade off on instruments.

Bringing English into the Mutley Chix fold was almost a no-brainer, remembers Lassen, because English was already a close friend to all of the Chix. English was a black woman who was born and raised in London, arriving in Gainesville via Jamaica and Fort Lauderdale. Mirroring the national punk rock scene (and no big surprise in north-central Florida), African Americans and other racial minorities were not well represented in the Gainesville punk scene. English, Troy Cook (who played in Young Pioneers with Greg Ceton and Mike Murphy) and Freddy the Bastard were among the only minorities to play major parts in the Gainesville punk scene in those early days.

Mutley Chix sent that first tape around to punk 'zines across the country and were getting positive feedback, including solid write-ups in *No Idea* and *Maximum Rocknroll*, one of the punk underground's most respected and long-running 'zines. The fan letters also started coming in.

Propelled by a small core of active organizers and musicians at its core, Gainesville's punk scene was growing (though it was in no danger of taking over the college rock and cover band scene that dominated the college town). Compared to bigger cities like Tampa and Miami, where the punk scenes were often more violent and dangerous, Gainesville's close-knit scene was gaining a reputation as one of the best in Florida.

# 5.

# DOLDRUMS EXPLODE

It wasn't long after Psychic Violents began their prolific visual and audio assault on Gainesville that another band popped up on the scene. Doldrums was the sharper, faster and more dangerous offspring of an earlier punk-ish and somewhat spacey band called Scared of Stares. The new band hit Gainesville like a bolt of lightning, pinning punk fans against the wall with the energy of their live shows.

Singer Peter Brightman moved to Gainesville in 1984 for college and immediately sought out the loudest music he could find. He had discovered punk rock a couple of years earlier during a family vacation to Berkeley, California, where he visited Rasputin Records.

"I saw the Dead Kennedys' *In God We Trust* album cover and I was like, 'Oh wow, somebody's really thinking the way I think.' I mean it was just perfect timing for me—I had a lot of anger, a lot of disgust…some of it was coming from the outside and some of it was coming from the inside," Brightman says.

Brightman's anger was the perfect fuel for Gainesville's punk scene.

"The whole Reagan era…I felt like there was a lot of ignorance, just the American culture to me was just sort of reduced down to this really driven-by-greed and superficial kind of shit and a lot of stupidity and this sort of frat boy mentality and the president was like this revered guy and he was just a piece of shit," Brightman says.

Brightman got involved in several short-lived projects, including one with Chad Salter (the early Roach Motel drummer and future Neurosis guitarist) and a band called The Ranch Hands with George Tabb. In 1985, he found a steadier musical outlet as the singer for Scared of Stares, which also included drummer Victor Wilkinson and guitarist Russell Johnson, who had played together for the first time in the short-lived Swamp Medicine with Charles Pinion.

Unlike so many of the punk kids and musicians in the Gainesville scene at the time, Wilkinson and Johnson were local kids. They didn't move to town for an education; Johnson had grown up just north of Gainesville in the tiny rural community of Live Oak, and Wilkinson grew up in east Gainesville, raised by his great-grandparents in the poorest part of town. They were Florida boys who grew up in the country, not on the coast.

After playing together for about a year, Scared of Stares shuffled a couple of members out, brought in a new bass player named Greg Pierce and dubbed themselves Doldrums. The ousted Scared of Stares members, Paul Spanbauer and Greg Drais, went on to form Target Practice with John McGuigan.

If Psychic Violents expanded the notion of punk and hardcore to encompass jangling guitar riffs, a touch of theatricality and more emphasis on melody, Doldrums zeroed in on hardcore's lightning speed and aggression and added precision riffs, a shifting and driving rhythm section and a dynamic, crazed frontman with melody, to boot.

Brightman looked like the all-American kid—long blond hair, handsome features, piercing blue eyes and a mischievous smile. But when he held a mic, something transformed in him. Brightman said that during those days, he felt more comfortable when he was on stage than he did in his regular life. That anger and disgust took over and found an outlet, and Brightman was the willing conduit.

"Pete Brightman was a riveting frontman," remembers Tom Nordlie. "[He] was charismatic and wild-eyed and looked like he was about three shots of Jack Daniel's away from killing somebody and made me feel [like], 'damn, stay out of that guy's way.'"

Nordlie succinctly describes Doldrums as one part Bad Brains and one part Motörhead. He describes the duo of Johnson and Wilkinson this way: "[Johnson] and Vic [Wilkinson] pretty much set forth a whole new rock-and-roll archetype—the good ol' boys who looked and talked and acted like car mechanics and were peerless heavy rock musicians once they got onstage… outgoing, friendly guys who loved rock-and-roll. And when they got onstage they were gods. Seriously."

Doldrums held Gainesville's growing punk underground at rapt attention. They were thought by many to be the band from Gainesville's punk scene that would "make it."

Doldrums singer Peter Brightman in mid-jump during one of the band's notably intense performances. *Photograph by Hudson Luce.*

Doldrums took their first batch of songs to Greg Ceton and Mike Murphy to record on their four-track tape recorder and planned a tour up the East Coast. Brightman and crew took the masters to a studio that would dub the tapes for them, but the sound quality of the dubbed tapes was not up to par, and the tapes turned out to be unusable. They resorted to dubbing them on a boombox while Brightman took care of packaging, printing, cutting out the covers and assembling the tapes. Wilkinson remembers the band dubbing those tapes and screen-printing T-shirts in the back of the van on the way to shows during the tour. The high-pitched "chipmunk" dubbing sound is still burned in his memory. "Goddamn I never want to hear that sound again," he says.

The members of Doldrums differed from their predecessors in Roach Motel or Mutley Chix in that they weren't particularly good at networking in the punk underground or forging relationships with other bands. Where other bands would hook up with musicians on tour or through correspondence, Doldrums largely remained isolated from the greater punk scene of the day. "We kind of tended to stay by ourselves. I don't know why but that's just how it was. I think the four of us were all sort of loners in our own right, so I think we were a bit of a loner band in a way," Brightman says.

At times, the band members tended to even keep away from each other. Although Wilkinson and Johnson were always close friends, tensions could

A flyer advertising a show with Chicago punk legends Naked Raygun, with Gainesville's Doldrums and Raging Pus Bags. *Courtesy of Ken Coffelt.*

run high in the band, sometimes resulting in the members not speaking outside of practices or performances. Brightman and Wilkinson both remember the tension and acknowledge that their own personal struggles and band turmoil could have very well contributed to their explosive live sets. But there was no denying their talents.

"We practiced a lot, and I think that's really important. And I think that's what distinguished us. I think separately we were all good at what we did and put it together, and you just rehearse until you're so sick of it that you just want to throw up," Brightman says.

By this time, Mutley Chix founding member Cindy Frey had left the band to relocate to San Franciso and was replaced by new bassist Pam Gauthier. And Psychic Violents' original drummer Dave Dickey left the band, replaced by Bill "BeeWee" White. Dickey, a born-again Christian, parted ways with the band because he was not always comfortable with Pinion's decidedly non-Christian lyrics. To accommodate Dickey, Pinion had even altered the lyrics to one song, "Leather Jesus," which imagined an S&M relationship with Christ, to a new song called "Happy Man." There were no hard feelings on either side; Dickey would even come back to play an occasional set with the Violents.

With new drummer White on board, Psychic Violents recorded an album with Ceton and Murphy called *Walk on Water*—a title they might not have gotten away with had Dickey remained in the band. And Mutley Chix recorded their second album, *True Grits*, a solid rollicking rock-and-punk document that exhibited their increasing musicianship and songwriting skills.

Between Mutley Chix, Psychic Violents, Doldrums and other bands like Young Pioneers, Raging Pus Bags and Naiomi's Hair (which would later relocate to Orlando), Gainesville's underground punk scene was thriving in the mid- to late 1980s.

Pinion took note of what he saw as a singular punk rock scene firing on all cylinders and began to record shows on the camcorder his father had recently given him. As an artist, he was always looking for new ways and mediums to express himself. He mulled over what to do with all the footage he was gathering. He had also recently decided to move to New York, where a lot of his artist friends lived, which meant Psychic Violents would be disbanding by the end of 1987. But before Pinion said goodbye to Florida, he wanted to make a hybrid farewell note/document of the Gainesville underground scene.

Pinion got together with buddies Steve Antczak and James C. "Hawk" Bassett, and a proposed rockumentary quickly evolved into a fictional "psycho-punk splatter-comedy" called *Twisted Issues*. Pinion recruited his friends and fellow Gainesville musicians to star in what would become something of a cult hit.

The surreal movie involves several groups of punks and skateboarders in Gainesville, including Pinion and his girlfriend, who repeatedly kill each other (and themselves), only to come back to life each time. The main plot follows a group of punks who accidentally kill a young skateboarder (interestingly, the only straight-edge character in the movie). The skateboarder comes back to life and terrorizes the punks until he is defeated by Hawk.

*Twisted Issues* serves as a solid document of what the mid-'80s Gainesville punk scene looked and sounded like. Live performances by Mutley Chix, Doldrums and Psychic Violents can all be seen in the movie. The soundtrack comprised Gainesville bands, including Mutley Chix, Doldrums, thrash metal band Hellwitch, Young Pioneers, Cindy Brady's Lisp, Just Demigods, Psychic Violents, Officer Friendly and the Bill Perry Orchestra. You can see Peter Brightman and Vic Wilkinson playing closeted gay lovers, Tom Nordlie as a bizarre newscaster and Mutley Chix performing at a house show. There's even a shot in the movie of a young Var Thelin and Ken Coffelt at the Mutley Chix show.

# 6.
# NO IDEA'S FIRST RECORD

Thelin, Coffelt and crew were still plugging away at the *No Idea* 'zine. Issue No. 5 came out in January 1988. With each issue becoming larger and more polished, *No Idea's* circulation would be up to two thousand by the end of the year, and it was now nationally distributed in alternative record stores.

Meanwhile, the writer Tom Nordlie—an avid metal fan and big supporter of the local music scene—had made it his unofficial mission to sing the praises of the Gainesville underground scene far and wide. He got a gig writing for *Creem* magazine when he saw that they had a new spinoff magazine called *Creem Thrash Metal*. In March 1988, Nordlie's glowing scene report about Gainesville was published, including write-ups raving about the recently disbanded Psychic Violents, Doldrums, Mutley Chix, Hellwitch and more. The article was one of the most widely distributed and earliest to shine a light on Gainesville's music underground.

Thelin had also begun kicking around the idea of releasing a seven-inch record through *No Idea*. He sought advice on how to go about pressing a record from some of the labels and individuals he looked up to in the punk community, including Washington, D.C.'s Dischord and its founder, Ian MacKaye.

"Ian was always really supportive back in the '80s. He always would drop me a postcard, that kind of thing. So yeah, I talked to him on the phone a couple of times because I didn't know what to do at a point....He's always given us lots of really good advice," Thelin says.

With a little bit of direction and some money he had saved, Thelin approached Doldrums about putting out the first No Idea seven-inch.

The band was excited about the idea and went into the studio and came out with the four songs that would be included on the record: "Believe," "Stabilizer," "Conquer the Fear" and "A Place to Hang Your Head." The record accompanied *No Idea* 'zine No. 6.

But, between recording the seven-inch and the release of No Idea Records No. 1, Doldrums came to an abrupt end. Interpersonal conflicts within the band finally came crashing in, and just like that, on the precipice of a national audience, they were done.

"I think the four of us were each individually really crazy people—especially at that time in our lives—and none of us had the correct coping skills to deal with what we had to deal with and it just fucking imploded," Brightman says.

Even the Doldrums interview that was included in the accompanying issue of *No Idea* is prefaced with a note saying that the band had likely broken up for good: "It is a touchy and unfortunate subject, but one that had to be discussed." The band members were even interviewed separately (with the exception of the duo of Johnson and Wilkinson, who were interviewed together). The bittersweet dynamic of being in a kickass band releasing their first record, but prematurely breaking up, is evident from all the members. They talk about how well the band had been received on tour and, strictly looking at the band's trajectory, how great things had been going. But it was all balanced by the fact that they were 99 percent sure they would never play together again. "It just sucks that we're not playing right now. A lot of people liked us," Wilkinson said in the interview.

By the end of the decade, with the demise of Doldrums and a lack of reliable venues, the punk scene in Gainesville would retreat into the shadows a bit, evolve and eventually reemerge as a whole new force in Gainesville. The *No Idea* 'zine was still growing and becoming more refined with each issue, but the original punk kids in town were getting older and drifting toward heavier music or more straightforward rock. In the meantime, a proto-grunge underground was rising from what was once the punk scene. Where Black Flag or the Minutemen were common touchstones, Gainesville musicians were now drawing inspiration from Black Sabbath, The Melvins and heavy experimental sounds being released on Amphetamine Reptile Records. For some, punk rock had become kids' stuff.

Mutley Chix carried on, the last one standing in the first wave of punk bands inspired by Roach Motel. But singer Sharon Lassen moved to Portland in 1989, yet again forcing the Chix to redefine themselves. The second record put out by No Idea Records was a split seven-inch featuring Mutley Chix and Bay Area band Crimpshrine. They brought saxophonist and vocalist Suzy Solgot into the band before recording their final album, *Burn Your Bra*.

As always, the term "punk" is problematic and amorphous. For the most part, the bands populating the underground scene in Gainesville in the late 1980s and early '90s were a far cry from the youthful hardcore of Roach Motel. Like the national trend, Gainesville bands were drawing inspiration from record labels like the grungy Sup Pop and groups like Mudhoney, Jesus Lizard and Butthole Surfers. (In fact, an article about the Mutley Chix in *The Alligator* refers to them as Gainesville's grunge queens, and Tom Nordlie used the term several times in his writing in the late '80s to describe Gainesville bands.) The product was bands like the heavy and sludgy post–Psychic Violents projects from Sam Gough, Carpet Farmers and Schlong—the latter still renowned as one of Gainesville's best early heavy bands. Grinch was another notable heavy punk-metal crossover, and Jorge Cervera formed Strongbox with Chad Salter. Others like Number 2 spread into country and jam territory, resembling an even more spacy Dinosaur jr.

Wilkinson and Johnson continued as a musical team, forming Stabilizer with Brent Wilson, a Miami transplant about ten years younger than his new bandmates. The band didn't have a long lifespan, but it managed to open for Fugazi when they played at the American Legion Hall, and they were included on No Idea's third seven-inch record along with Boston ska band Bim Skala Bim. Wilson had also played in a metal-punk hybrid called Corrupture. Being much younger than many in the Gainesville scene at the time, Wilson was more interested in playing faster, more straightforward punk, so he split off from Corrupture, whose members would later evolve into Grinch.

The Stabilizer/Bim Skala Bim split accompanied *No Idea* 'zine No. 8, which was also the first appearance of the simple but memorable Stressface logo that would come to be closely associated with No Idea Records (at the time, the grimacing face wore a top hat and bow tie, which eventually went away). Thelin had made the sketch one day at work in an attempt to remember a character he and Ken Coffelt used to draw named "Amazingly Boy."

Tom Nordlie's Turbo Satan was known for their wild live antics. He describes the joke-y metal band as GWAR on a $200 budget. Nordlie's other band, Butter the Heifer, however, carried on the punk spirit of late-era Black Flag. (Nordlie also had a stint playing Velvet Underground songs with the band's drummer, Maureen Tucker, and played in a short-lived Gainesville band called Die Trying, whose drummer, Todd Barry, would go on to national fame as a standup comedian.)

Coffelt eventually fell away from No Idea to pursue other projects, but Thelin was still pushing to keep the punk rock scene in Gainesville vital, booking bands and putting out issues of *No Idea*.

By the end of the 1980s, Thelin had basically already moved away from Gainesville in his mind. The several years that separated him and the older punk crew in Gainesville always made him feel like a bit of an outsider, and the amount of flak he had to take from locals who felt that their bands, or their friends' bands, weren't getting the proper coverage by the (now national) *No Idea* 'zine was growing tiresome. Thelin had also sought to open his own music venue, but the proposition fell through.

But the real kicker was that the music scene wasn't doing it for him anymore. The youthful vitality and punk vigor that dominated the mid-1980s had faded away. With trends turning toward the sludgier pre-grunge of bands like Schlong and Grinch, Thelin had his eyes on places like Washington, D.C., and the San Francisco Bay Area, whose punk scene was exploding with bands like Crimpshrine, Green Day and Jawbreaker. Thelin had visited both cities at that point; he was planning to move to one of the two destinations within the next year or two, after he had saved up enough money at his screen-printing job.

# PART II

# THE LIFTING, 1989–1999

# 7.

# GAINESVILLE PUNK FINDS A HOME

Thanks to a handful of active bands and the growing distribution of the *No Idea* fanzine, Gainesville gained a reputation within the state for its punk scene, even if it looked to some like its glory days were in the past. But a new generation of bands and venues would revitalize the scene in a big way, sparking momentum that would carry through to the new millennium. While the nation was looking to Seattle and the grunge-alternative-punk explosion, Gainesville was learning to wield its punk in a different way—catchier, wittier, more passionate and brimming with melody.

Throughout much of the 1980s, like so many small towns in the United States, Gainesville's downtown was a largely unkempt grid of neglected buildings, having been abandoned by its more-affluent denizens for newer and "safer" parts of town. The end of the decade saw the tide turning as developments like the Sun Center slowly began attracting more affluent businesses back to the area. When an old building on Southeast First Street that previously housed a martial arts studio went up for sale in the heart of the dilapidated downtown area, it caught the attention of twenty-nine-year-old Alan Bushnell. The Bushnell family had recently inherited a sum of money from Alan's grandmother, and he was looking for an investment. He talked his family into going in with him to purchase the deserted building and another larger one that stood next to it.

Bushnell was a quiet, unassuming character, but he had a passion for live music of all types. He had been going to shows in Gainesville since he moved to town in 1977 and was a musician himself, playing guitar in bands ranging from country to rock to new wave. He was disappointed that Gainesville couldn't seem to hang on to a club that specialized in original music and saw the cover band scene as just more rehashed, warmed-over radio rock played with less talent. When he saw the building on Southeast First Street, he decided to do something about the problem.

Bushnell's vision for the small building would combine his dream of providing a place for bands to play original music with the more stable business plan of opening a used bookstore and lunch counter to bring in most of the cash flow. It would be called The Hardback Café, after the books lining the walls. With the help of his sister Tina, Alan opened the new business in the spring of 1989 to little fanfare. Used books adorned shelves, and a meager menu offered lunch to the sparse downtown crowd and college kids looking for a mid-afternoon beer. Not long after The Hardback opened, Bushnell planned a grand opening celebration, booking for his very first show a jammy local band called The Tone Unknown.

The popular group happened to feature a drummer named Rob McGregor, who would go on to become The Hardback's primary sound

A photograph of The Hardback Café at night, taken from the second-floor steps of the Hippodrome State Theatre across the street. *Photograph by Tim Hill.*

58

engineer and an essential part of the Gainesville punk scene. McGregor remembers that very first Hardback show well; it set a precedent for the years to come. "It was off the charts, it was wild and crazy." He also recalls The Hardback's efforts as a bookstore: "Crickets…"

McGregor says The Tone Unknown was asked back to play again, and the band let The Hardback keep the admission money from the door. It wasn't long before the bookshelves began fading into the background and The Hardback's role as a music venue came to the forefront.

From the beginning, Bushnell's only rule for The Hardback was that bands had to play original music; no cover bands allowed. It didn't take long for hungry bands in town to start migrating to The Hardback. It quickly became the go-to venue for music of all kinds, as long as it wasn't covers. Gainesville had a robust college and indie rock scene at the time, and bands like NDolphin and Aleka's Attic (featuring an up-and-coming actor named River Phoenix, whose family lived in nearby Micanopy, on guitar and vocals) found a home at The Hardback.

Not booking cover bands was perplexing for some, particularly the music publishing companies that normally billed music venues for royalties on copyrighted songs played by the cover bands they assumed populated the monthly calendars. But not at The Hardback. Bushnell says ASCAP and BMI would send him bills and harass him in the early days, even sending in spies to see if a band was playing cover songs. After about a year, they finally gave up, and Bushnell never heard from them again.

The one cultural bright spot in crumbling downtown Gainesville in the '80s was the Hippodrome Theatre, which stood directly across the street from The Hardback. The Hippodrome, a playhouse founded in 1971, frequently hosted performances by local and touring theater companies. Unfortunately, the noise from The Hardback quickly became an issue for the Hippodrome and its playgoers. Desperate to reach a resolution, Bushnell proposed that The Hardback shows would not start until 10:00 p.m.; by that time the Hippodrome plays would have ended. Everyone agreed to the solution, and a trend of late-night shows began in Gainesville that runs to this day. With the first band on any given night at The Hardback starting at 10:00 (and, in reality, usually later), shows would sometimes run until 3:00 or 4:00 a.m.

In addition to NDolphin and Aleka's Attic, popular locals like Schlong, Grinch, Bumble and the Carpet Farmers also found a welcome home at the little dive bar with the low, lattice-worked ceiling. Although many of those early regular Hardback bands drew some kind of inspiration from punk rock, the more traditional punk sound—the enthusiasm, energy and melody—was for the most part still being scoffed at by the older crowd.

One of the few bands playing poppy, energetic punk was the short-lived Jeffersons, a unique band in Gainesville at the time. The band's most active period only lasted for about a year, between the summer of 1990 and 1991, but they left a mark, helping to inspire a group of young punk fans who had just hit town and were looking to create their own scene.

Patrick Hughes, a Gainesville native and author who ran a record store in town in the '90s, says that when they were at their best, the Jeffersons were a cross between The Ramones, New York Dolls and The Fall. And their live shows at The Hardback left an impression that remains, more than twenty years later. "There's dudes in dresses rolling around on the floor playing these Johnny Thunders guitar licks and screaming right in your face and dancing around," Hughes says.

While the Jeffersons' time as a band was brief, their straightforward, hooky punk foreshadowed the sound that would soon redefine Gainesville's punk scene.

As always, UF continued to draw students from all over the state of Florida. By 1990, a younger and enthusiastic group of punk kids was moving into town. They were punks who cut their teeth on issues of *No Idea*, were eager to get their hands on any new punk music they could find and shared many of the same musical tastes as Var Thelin. Perhaps most important, they weren't burdened with the cool cynicism of the older crowd. Groups of kids from Orlando, Miami and Tampa would give the staggering Gainesville punk scene a huge and much-needed jolt. If Gainesville wasn't the punk rock mecca the new kids imagined it to be when they arrived, they soon turned it into one, with the help of two bands in particular: Spoke and Radon.

# 8.

# SPOKE AND RADON USHER IN A NEW ERA

A young Orlando transplant named Jon Resh had moved to Gainesville in
1988. Although he had discovered punk back in his high school days,
he spent his first couple of years at UF mostly holed up in his dorm room,
strumming away at his cheap Ibanez Roadster guitar, played through a tiny,
trebly practice amp. Like Thelin, he wasn't into the apathetic heaviness that
was taking hold in Gainesville, but he did find kinship in bands like the
Jeffersons, Stabilizer, Naiomi's Hair and Strongbox (yet another Cervera
project). Also like Thelin, he was inspired by the Gilman Street scene in
Berkeley; Washington, D.C.'s angular and emotional hardcore; and bands
like Hüsker Dü, Sonic Youth and Naked Raygun.

In the fall of 1990, Resh brought up the prospect of starting a band with
two of his best friends from Orlando, Chuck Horne and Scott Huegel. The
latter had recently joined Resh in Gainesville to attend UF, and Horne was
happy to get out of Orlando for the prospect of playing music with friends.
Resh would sing and play guitar, Horne would play drums and Huegel would
play bass (which he did not yet know how to play). They would be called
Spoke; Resh liked the name because it was short and punchy, and Horne
and Huegel had no arguments. Resh had a handful of songs already written,
and they quickly went to work turning them into full band arrangements.

Spoke's original goal was simply to play a show. Like Resh, Huegel was not
on board with the direction the Gainesville scene had taken in recent years.
Huegel remembers the proto-grunge, punk offshoot that had taken hold
in Gainesville as having a distinct hippie vibe, complete with lots of noodle

dancing at shows. Huegel and Resh both say the scene they walked into could be described in one word: patchouli. Spoke wanted to do something different.

It wasn't long before Spoke had lined up their first three shows. An excited Resh put up a flyer in The Hardback featuring an image by French photographer Henri Cartier-Bresson of two dogs having sex on the street. It was taken down in short time by Bushnell. Resh recounts in his excellent band memoir, *Amped*, that after going on a tirade to Bushnell about First Amendment rights, Bushnell replied, "It's got nothing to do with censorship. It's grossing out customers during lunch. They say they can't eat while looking at a couple of dogs fucking."

Spoke's very first show was at the dingy Club Gravity. Resh writes that it was populated by a decent crowd of friends and curious music fans. But with a new band's usual hiccups brought about by nerves and self-consciousness, Spoke wasn't exactly embraced as Gainesville's new punk-rock saviors. But Resh recalls some friendly heckling from the crowd—a veiled compliment in Gainesville. Heckling means they're paying attention; silence means they couldn't care less.

Their second show was at The Hardback. The seeds Resh and friends were planting were finding fresh soil into which they could dig deep and thrive

One of Spoke's early performances. *Courtesy of Jon Resh.*

for years to come. Spoke quickly shed the stage jitters and became the new torchbearers for Gainesville punk rock. Their shows were almost as much about goofing around on stage, and with the crowd, as they were about the music.

Spoke's music was an amalgamation of Resh, Huegel and Horne's musical influences pared down to a sharp attack of power chords, melodic choruses and an underlying unquantifiable passion. Shades of D.C. post-hardcore bands like Rites of Spring or Embrace can be heard at times, while Resh's voice might soar with Naked Raygun's Jeff Pezzati's infectious melodies or recall the hazy, deadpan catchiness of Dinosaur jr.'s J Mascis. Like so many memorable bands, the passion is what made Spoke stand out. It didn't matter if they played three distorted chords for three minutes straight—the energy and genuine nature of the music made people take notice. The most well-trained classical pianist can play any sheet of music with the careful precision of a surgeon's scalpel, but Jerry Lee Lewis banged the keys so hard he made girls pass out.

Resh says, "I honestly feel like any real power we had in what we did was really just the intensity with which we brought our enthusiasm to playing and whatnot, not necessarily the music itself."

Thelin had become friends with Resh while running in the very small punk circle in Gainesville in the late '80s. But when Spoke began to play out, Thelin saw something—a spark that would ignite the very scene he was planning on moving away to find.

Their live shows were not only defined by youthful energy, but Spoke's lack of cynicism made each show a party. Resh would punctuate the time between songs with witty, funny banter, and the band members would throw "party favors" into the audience—candy, flour, pasta, whatever they could find. They would also bring people up to play with them. The atmosphere was a breath of fresh air for the other young punk fans who had recently moved to town, and it inspired and propelled them to start their own bands.

"Jon was such a magnetic personality," says Thelin. "He had the gift of gab…and he was able to bring disparate people together. So because of him being a magnet for all this, him starting a band with all of his friends, them learning to play…and then their friends' bands, and people they're friends with, they started bands, and then lots of bands were happening, all with the same kind of enthusiasm."

The exterior of SpokeHouse. *Courtesy of Jon Resh.*

Spoke's music was one thing, but another essential element of the Gainesville punk scene at the time, besides the burgeoning Hardback, was SpokeHouse (Resh wrote the dwelling's name out as one word in *Amped*, so I'll do the same here). SpokeHouse was an unassuming, run-down house built in the 1920s that had been divided into apartment units, located a block from the UF campus.

Resh was the first member of Spoke to move into the old house. His bandmates moved in over time; within a couple of years, all of the "normal" tenants had moved away, and SpokeHouse was populated entirely by raucous, energetic punks. SpokeHouse was a hotbed for all punk activities in Gainesville and many, many late-night antics. Resh writes that, at one point, SpokeHouse was home to three bands, "nine fanzines, three small record labels and a record/zine distributor."

"You were surrounded by like-minded people 24/7," Huegel says. "More often than not it was just pure fun....We were caught up in this inertia of having a great time coupled with creativity, so it was a very fecund environment for that kind of stuff."

It was also the birthplace of "pastacore"—a silly in-joke that defined the youthful scene without actually being a definable word. Like the Descendents' philosophy of "All," it was a particular mindset that you either got or you didn't. In the chapter of *Amped* titled "pastacore," Resh offers a long list of what constitutes pastacore, from eating a bunch of cheap pasta and "falling asleep from the pasta buzz" to "scoring a near-mint condition LP by Devo, the Germs, Chrome or Token Entry for three dollars in the Hyde and Zeke's 'new used' vinyl bin" and "making up crazy new dances at Pat Hughes' Funkadelic Dance Parties." Every description of pastacore basically boils down to an idea or experience that captures the thrill of carefree youth and being smart enough to savor those moments.

Just down the street from SpokeHouse was the Barcelona House. While the former was primarily occupied by folks who had moved from the Orlando area or were otherwise associated with the growing number of Orlando-affiliated bands, the Barcelona House represented the Miami constituent. The close proximity of two houses full of energetic punks with a lot of free time resulted in more than a few fireworks wars between the two groups.

The *No Idea* fanzine and micro record label carried on through what Thelin remembers as slim years for Gainesville punk. But when Spoke and all of its associated momentum burst onto the scene in 1991, Thelin was infused with new energy. The previous year, Thelin had released the very first No Idea record not accompanied by an issue of the fanzine, but it had turned out to be a bit of a dud. Thelin said the band, Crankshaft, was basically a clone of every San Francisco Bay Area band he loved at the time mashed into one. He was excited to release their music, but by the time he got to work with them, they had evolved into a funk band.

"I haven't listened to that record in years. I'm sure I would cringe and think it was funny if I listened to it now," says Thelin.

But Spoke now had Thelin's attention, and it was an added bonus that he was friends with the band. Spoke soon headed to Tallahassee to record with Tommy Hamilton, who had played in the hardcore band (and Roach Motel peers) Hated Youth before moving toward more metal projects. Spoke's four-song seven-inch *Celebrated* came out as No Idea Records No. 5.

While Spoke was the early torchbearer energizing the new generation of Gainesville punk bands and fans, the band that formed just on their heels fanned those flames into a full-on inferno. They were called Radon.

After Stabilizer dissolved, Brent Wilson, like Thelin, felt adrift in the proto-grunge-punk-hippie scene the older fans were now into. One of the reasons Stabilizer split up was because Wilson craved the youthful energy of a punk direction while Victor Wilkinson and Russ Johnson were gravitating toward straightforward rock.

Wilson found the punk direction he was looking for when Dave Rohm, whom he knew from Miami, asked him to check out some songs he had been working on. Wilson was interested before he even heard the songs, because he had been a fan of Rohm's high school punk band, Minimum Wage. Rohm had also been in Gainesville for a couple of years by this time, but he had kept a low profile while focusing on his studies at UF.

The son of a music professor, Rohm had been playing guitar since he was ten years old. When Rohm knew that his dad was going to buy him his first guitar, he envisioned rocking out on a Gibson SG like Angus Young from AC/DC. Instead, he got a nylon-string classical guitar and was enrolled in lessons and held to a three-times-per-week-at-minimum practice schedule. Although he had years of technical training behind him, by the time Rohm was in college, his musical tastes were firmly planted in the worlds of punk and underground music. And he took notice of the changing winds in Gainesville with bands like the Jeffersons and Spoke.

Rohm recalls going to that very first Spoke show and coming out inspired, thinking, "*I can do that.*"

Finding a drummer can be the trickiest part of starting a new band, and Rohm and Wilson, eager to get started on their new project, found themselves in this common predicament. They did know of an available drummer named Bill Clower, however, who was a bit younger and had gone to their same high school. But he still lived in Miami. When Rohm got word that Clower was coming up to Gainesville to visit his girlfriend at the time, he says:

> *I secretly sabotaged him and brought my amp in the car and my guitar. Somebody had a drum set* [available], *and I was like, "Hey, I heard you play drums," and made him play with me. And as soon as I played some songs that I'd written that he had never heard in his life, like "Facial Disobedience," it was like he knew the entire song. He totally spoke the language.*

Clower eventually moved to Gainesville, and by August 1991, Radon was officially a band. Rohm and Wilson both brought songs to the table that they had been working on. After just a few practices, Rohm got wind of a house show where they would jump on the bill for their debut. The next big goal was to play The Hardback.

HELP ELIMINATE HUNGER IN GAINESVILLE

# B E N E F I T
*for the St. Francis House at*

# CLUB VELVET
## Saturday, March 28

WITH:

**G R I N C H**
**R A D O N**
**S P O K E**
**BOMBSHELL**
**WORDSWORTH**
**POSTAGE PAID**

*cost of admission:*
# 2 CANS OF FOOD

❥*Cans will be taken at the door and donated to the St. Francis House* ❥
**SHOW BEGINS AT 9:30 p.m.** — **AND WE MEAN IT.**

HEY! — We need help moving cans, working the door, putting up fliers, etc. If you want to participate, please call Jonathan at 338-1489. *Viva Pastacore!*

A flyer advertising a benefit show for the St. Francis House. *Courtesy of Matt Sweeting.*

"We played a couple of house parties and worked up the nerve to go talk to Alan at The Hardback," Rohm says. "He was so cool to us....We opened for Bumble, and he liked us. He actually took the time to listen to us and knew it enough to know he liked it and continued to book us."

Like Spoke, it wasn't long before Radon headed to Tommy Hamilton's in Tallahassee for their first recording, which would become No Idea Records No. 6—a self-titled seven-inch with two of Rohm's songs, "Radon" and "Facial Disobedience," and two of Wilson's songs, "Welcome Home" and "Exhaustra."

The one-two punch of the Spoke and Radon seven-inches from No Idea created new momentum for the tiny label and was a huge inspiration for many punk bands in town. To see their friends' bands have an actual, tangible record was a big deal.

Like Spoke, Radon's music was a breath of fresh air at the time, and the Gainesville punk scene responded en masse. Even Radon's earliest shows were chaotic affairs. Rohm said that, prior to their official Radon seven-inch being released, they had recorded demo versions of the songs to cassette and given them to their friends, so most of the scene knew the music well enough to sing along from the very first shows.

Rob McGregor, who was working sound at The Hardback by then, says, "I'd never seen crowds go that nuts before, with Radon they just went fucking nuts—I mean it was crazy."

All of a sudden the tiny, close-knit punk scene seemed flooded with new fans. Hundreds of people would show up to The Hardback to watch Radon, filling the tiny venue beyond capacity. Influential 'zine authors and traveling punks like Aaron Cometbus and Dishwasher Pete would come through town to see the band. Radon was in the ether in Gainesville. Regular college kids

Radon performing at The Hardback. *Courtesy of Brent Wilson.*

who weren't even familiar with punk rock would show up, just because they heard it was the place to be.

There was no denying Radon's hold on the Gainesville punk scene in the early '90s.

Radon's music tended to be a mix of two different punk styles. There were Rohm songs, and there were Wilson songs. Rohm songs were a wash of jangly yet aggressive guitars that recalled Hüsker Dü but with a distinct rhythm that set things a little askew until Rohm's infectious vocals pulled it all into a focused center. In a way, Wilson songs were the opposite. Metal-influenced guitar riffs drive the songs while Wilson's vocals wash over them before culminating in big, catchy choruses. Clower was a forceful presence behind it all, propelling all the songs with intensity and precision.

The two styles worked together because Radon songs as a whole, whether by Rohm or Wilson, had a seething, aggressive energy with just the right amount of misanthropic melancholy lurking under the surface. It was deceptively dark and angry music that happened to be some of the catchiest punk rock of the era.

Even the band's very first song on their seven-inch (also called "Radon) is a revenge fantasy about a female superhero named Radon in which Rohm sings of sheets covered in blood ("Tye dye the whites red!"). With one of the band's most infectious choruses, "Radon" essentially became the band's calling card as Rohm's vocals during live shows would be overtaken by the crowd shouting the chorus, "Bow down to me, bow down to me. Radon, Radon, Radon, Radon!"


Between 1991 and 1993, Spoke and Radon were the bands to be in Gainesville. And The Hardback or house shows were the places to find them. They led a very fertile period for Gainesville punk. It was a time of transition not only in the Gainesville underground but across the country as elements of various influential subcultures seeped into popular culture. Nirvana's *Nevermind* had come out in September 1991, and "grunge" and "alternative" music was bursting full force into the mainstream. Punk fans who got beat up for wearing Nirvana T-shirts when the band's debut album *Bleach* came out were now getting high fives from the same people for wearing *Nevermind* shirts.

Spoke continued honing their exuberant live shows, playing in Gainesville whenever they could and venturing to Orlando and Miami, sometimes with Radon. But having reached their initial goal of actually playing a show and

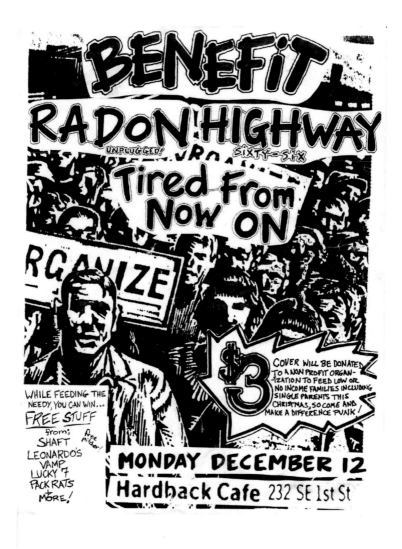

A flyer advertising a benefit show at The Hardback, with Radon, Highway 66 and Tired From Now On. *Courtesy of Matt Sweeting.*

having the added bonus of the No Idea seven-inch, Spoke decided to book a Southeast tour.

Huegel said they used to send their music to college radio stations, especially the towns they knew they would stop at on tour. The band soon developed a friendship with a college radio DJ in Columbia, South Carolina. He was friendly and seemed like he was into their music, but in those pre-Internet days, there wasn't a way for a small band to tell if they were making an impact in any given place. But when Spoke showed up at their gig in Columbia, there was a huge crowd of people lined up to see them play.

"We got on stage and there were a couple hundred kids there," Huegel says. "[We] started playing, I look out and people are singing along to our songs—they knew our songs, and that's when I was really hooked…not because of the ego but just the fact that wow, we're doing this man, look at this, we're making a connection here—this is connecting with people."

Spoke continued to tour over the next year, striking up friendships with bands like Jawbox and Shudder to Think and releasing seven-inches and compilation tracks along the way.

In Gainesville, it seemed like new punk bands were forming weekly. Gainesville's incestuous scene, where one musician might be in three or four different bands, often with the same mix of people, kicked into high gear. Thelin was even inspired during this fertile time to pick up his bass guitar to play in a band called Bombshell, while other bands like Highway 66, Pasteeater, Moonraker, Grain, When Puberty Strikes, Don's Ex-Girlfriend, King Friday, Clairmel, Wordsworth and tons more were all borne out of this era and proliferated during this time, helping to solidify Gainesville as one of the most active and influential punk scenes in the Southeast. And all of them

Danarchy, a staple of the Gainesville punk scene, crowd surfing at The Hardback. *Courtesy of Dave Rohm.*

were regulars at the anything-goes Hardback, where Alan Bushnell kept a steady hand at the wheel during some of the wildest nights imaginable.

Patrick Hughes, who was working at Hyde and Zeke's at the time, sums up how raucous things could get at The Hardback.

"Pung was playing, and people were lighting off bottle rockets and roman candles inside The Hardback," he recalls. Hughes said he lit a string of Black Cat firecrackers and stuck them in bass player Aaron Martin's back pocket and watched him spin around and around trying to find them as they burned through his jeans with every pop-pop-pop. While bottle rockets and flaming colored balls from the roman candles shot across the room, Hughes remembers looking over at Bushnell, "just pouring a beer and there were like flaming missiles behind the bar—he's just as placid as can be, pouring some of that shitty beer that gave us all wretched hangovers."

The Hardback had easily become the go-to bar for punk shows in those days, so when a new club called the Covered Dish opened a few blocks west of The Hardback in June 1992, the punks quickly drew battle lines. The Covered Dish was started by a young music fan and entrepreneur named Bill Bryson, who had moved from Chapel Hill, North Carolina, where he worked at the popular club Cat's Cradle. He wanted to open his own club similar to Cat's Cradle. After scoping out several towns, he settled on Gainesville.

The club had what most towns would be happy about—an owner and booker who was a huge music fan and ran the club in a professional and fair way. And most of the city of Gainesville was happy to attend shows at the Covered Dish. But the punk contingent was quickly calling Bryson a sellout, and the Covered Dish became known as the "corporate venue"—usually only until one of their own bands were asked to play there.

Bryson said the Covered Dish was never meant to be a punk clubhouse or even to compete with The Hardback. Bryson booked a variety of styles of music, national touring bands and also local bands that were more broadly appealing to more than just the punk crowd. Over time, and as more Hardback bands had a chance to interact with Bryson and his venue, the pushback against the Covered Dish lessened. As a punk or alternative music fan in the early 1990s, it would have been hard to boycott a club just down the road that was booking bands like Green Day, Jawbreaker, Archers of Loaf and Superchunk.

# 9.

# LESS THAN JAKE GROWS, SPOKE AND RADON CALL IT A DAY

Another band that cropped up during this time and would further boost Gainesville into the national spotlight was Less Than Jake. Chris DeMakes had left his high school band and good friend Vinnie Fiorello behind in Port Charlotte, Florida, when he moved to Gainesville for college. But when he got to town in 1992 and saw the punk scene blowing up, he called Fiorello and told him he needed to get to Gainesville so they could continue playing music.

While the origins of Less Than Jake were in Port Charlotte, the project was solidified once DeMakes (playing guitar and singing) and Fiorello (drums) were both in Gainesville and added Chris Campisi of Highway 66 on bass. Campisi was replaced early on by Roger Lima after DeMakes met him at a party and brought him in for a practice. The early version of Less Than Jake was a fairly straightforward presentation of pop punk. But, being influenced by the British punk band Snuff, they soon decided to add horns to their music and recruited Jessica Mills to play saxophone.

Less Than Jake quickly became a regular in the Gainesville punk scene. Thelin was an early fan, recognizing the band's talents and releasing their first seven-inch, *Smoke Spot*, as No Idea Records No. 12. But from the very beginning Less Than Jake stood apart from a lot of the other Gainesville bands, because their brand of punk was a little slicker, a little faster—less inspired by the Hüsker Düs or Naked Rayguns of the underground and taking cues from snottier West Coast punk acts like Operation Ivy or NOFX.

Less Than Jake performing on an early tour in Blacksburg, Virginia. The stage was too small for the whole band, so trombone player Buddy Schaub stands on a table next to the stage. *Photograph by David Woolfall.*

With the addition of Mills on saxophone and Buddy Schaub shortly thereafter on trombone, Less Than Jake's sound swiftly moved more toward a ska-punk hybrid. As they began to get more attention locally and fell more and more into the category of "ska band," Less Than Jake felt a distinct pushback from the Gainesville punk scene. They also practiced religiously and were seen by some members in the punk scene as "careerist," often (and often unfairly) a controversial aspiration in the punk scenes of the '90s.

"That definitely affected us," Schaub says. "It wasn't even because of success at first....It was because we were a ska band, and ska bands weren't cool."

Schaub said the negativity would get to him at times, but Fiorello, who also wrote the band's lyrics, always kept a positive attitude about things, pointing out all the fans that they did have and dismissing the naysayers. But a big boost of confidence for the band members came from the fact that some of Less Than Jake's earliest and biggest supporters were the guys in Spoke.

"I felt like sometimes we were the only ones—like Scott, Chuck and I—were the only ones that loved this band," Resh says. "We were like, why doesn't everybody else in the world dig what's happening here? It kind of freaked me out. I talked to Vinnie about it and I'd be like, man, just keep soldiering on because what you're doing is real and it's right and just, like I totally believed in them from the start."

Meanwhile, Spoke, Radon, No Idea Records, The Hardback and the surge of quality punk bands around town were bringing fresh recognition to Gainesville. Spoke's music had gotten generally good reviews in punk fanzines around the country, and they had gotten to tour the United States. In only two years, the band had released their *Celebrated* seven-inch and two follow-ups, *Visualize Industrial Collapse* and *Seratonin*, which were all eventually compiled onto a full-length CD from No Idea called *Done*. They would also release another full-length, *All We Need of Hell*, on Kung Fu Zombie and Allied Recordings. Kung Fu Zombie was a small label run by Patrick Hughes and his friend Mike Wohlgemuth; Allied Recordings was run by John Yates in San Francisco.

Allied, which also put out music by J Church, Buzzoven and Neurosis, was a big early supporter of No Idea and included Spoke and Radon on their compilations and put out a full-length by Bombshell. Thelin credits Yates and Allied as being instrumental in No Idea gaining traction in the national punk scene. Yates, who had an account with large independent distributor Mordam Records, allowed No Idea to use his account to press CDs, which gave the fledgling label much lower rates than Thelin would have otherwise been able to get.

Spoke was operating in the heyday of the alt-rock explosion in the United States; within their first year as a band, they had already gotten inquiries from several major labels that had read positive Spoke reviews in punk 'zines and asked the band to send in materials for the label to listen to. The band saw the majors as predators with dollar signs in their eyes, trolling through America's underground for the next Nirvana. Resh received one letter from MCA that he found particularly irritating. Instead of sending the requested copy of *Seratonin*, he stuffed the half-eaten peanut butter and jelly sandwich that was in his hand into an envelope and mailed it to the return address.

By the summer of 1993, Scott Huegel had graduated from the University of Florida and had been accepted into a program that would send him to Japan to teach English for two years. There was no way around it, Spoke was coming to an end. They played their final show on July 3, 1993, at The Hardback along with Pasteeater (also their last show), Ajo, Bombshell, Less Than Jake and Dig Doug.

Resh writes that with the 2:00 a.m. crowd throwing firecrackers, jumping all over the equipment and bumping into the band members, there was no hope of sounding good. But the point was to have a good time, and that they did. They were able to pull that passion out of themselves one last time. As Spoke smashed through "Muse," their final song, Resh writes, "As I screamed the chorus, my body was channeled into the furious sawing motion of my strumming arm, my pick bashing back and forth against the strings hard and fast like a piston. My head was spinning, my flesh chilled....Only this beautiful, unremitting noise seemed present and real."

Just like that, the band that had rallied Gainesville punk only two years earlier was gone for good.


But Radon still stood—at least for a little longer. Unlike Spoke, Radon had never played a show outside of Florida, although they were still drawing crowds of hundreds to their Gainesville shows and had a buzz in the national underground scene. They had recorded several seven-inches and contributed songs to various compilations in their two years together. They also recorded a full-length album with Rob McGregor (who had recently begun recording bands as a hobby) that, by a series of unfortunate circumstances, remained unreleased until about five years later.

But the beginning of the end for Radon came in early 1994. They were booked to play their very first out-of-Florida show in Chapel Hill, North Carolina, with respected indie rockers Archers of Loaf. It was an exciting opportunity for Radon. Archers of Loaf were at the forefront of the indie underground at the time, and Chapel Hill was their hometown. It was a big show.

The band members were driving up separately, with various friends making the trip with them. Dave Rohm was riding in the back seat of his friend's car. It wasn't long after they passed the North Carolina border that the driver swerved to miss some debris in the road and overcorrected, sending the car soaring off a highway embankment and slamming into a tree. Rohm and another friend were thrown from the car. Luckily, nobody was killed, but Rohm had a massive head injury, with lacerations all over his face. One half of his face eventually turned black.

Needless to say, Radon didn't get to play the big show that night, and Rohm was in the hospital for a week. Rohm says the only thing on the television in his room was a maternity channel. He was in a painkiller daze, watching videos of mothers and their newborn babies set to a backdrop of soothing music playing on a loop for twenty-four hours a day. Rohm says he began to have a change of heart about the road he felt he was heading down. His role as punk rock frontman had overshadowed the path he thought he would take in life. He began questioning how much longer he wanted to carry on in Radon.

"Bill and I had actually started working on booking a tour for Radon, and we were planning on going," Wilson says. "And we had that show with Archers of Loaf in Chapel Hill, and [the wreck] changed Dave's brain. And he'll be the first to tell you that, I think—the idea was in Dave's brain that the 'rock 'n' roll lifestyle' was going to kill him."

Radon carried on for a while longer, but later that year, Rohm decided to quit and pursue what he saw as a more traditional life trajectory.

By 1994, Spoke and Radon were both gone, only a couple of short years after they began. It marked the end of an era. Meanwhile, Less Than Jake was steadily on the rise. But, because of the pushback they got from the very beginning, they weren't positioned to carry the scene the way Spoke or Radon had—they were well on their way to the national stage.

While the end of Spoke and Radon marked a turning point for Gainesville punk, in the mid-'90s the town was about to see its most diverse, prolific and creative punk era to date.

# 10.

# GAINESVILLE PUNK EVOLVES

During the 1990s, punk rock in the United States was a nebulous beast, constantly evolving, pushing into new territory and sprouting subgenre after subgenre. Much like the genre's eclectic beginnings in the early to mid-'70s, there was no defining sound for the punk underground in the '90s.

While many had seen Nirvana's initial success as a victory for the punks, by April 1994, Kurt Cobain was dead, and in many ways, the punk underground had moved on from the band, since it no longer "belonged" to them. Also in 1994, Green Day's *Dookie* brought punk's most poppy and snotty elements to the masses. Based on that template, bands like The Offspring and Blink-182 would fit nicely into what the mainstream considered punk rock later in the decade. Each of those bands did emerge from punk's underground but only represented a small portion of the vast genre. (Incidentally, Green Day had played in Gainesville at The Hardback in 1990 and again at the Covered Dish in 1993 with Pasteeater; its members crashed on the floor at SpokeHouse. Scott Huegel recalls singer and guitarist Billie Joe Armstrong shooting bottle rockets out of his ass in the middle of the street that night.)

Back in the late 1980s, bands like Washington, D.C.'s Rites of Spring and Fugazi had helped establish the idea that a punk band didn't need to sound anything like the Sex Pistols, Minor Threat or anybody else for that matter. For those and many other bands, it was more about maintaining a DIY ethos and approaching true, honest artistic expression. Punk rock's bullshit detectors were on high alert throughout the '90s.

In Gainesville, while Spoke, Radon and others were deservedly at the top of the Gainesville punk hierarchy in the early 1990s, the fertile period they inspired helped the Gainesville scene truly explode into many directions.

Matt Sweeting had moved to Gainesville from Miami in 1992. After living in the dorms for a year, he moved into an old house a few blocks east of the UF campus. He didn't have many friends in the punk scene at the time, but he was able to start a heavy post-hardcore band called Utility. And with few connections in town, Sweeting didn't really know how to get his band on local shows, so he just started booking shows at his house, which was quickly named the Utility House.

The first shows at the Utility House didn't draw many people, however. Sweeting says it was always his band, Utility, with some other young punk band they could talk into playing the show. But the first "big" show they had was with Thelin's band Bombshell and Less Than Jake—their first show with Jessica Mills on saxophone. Sweeting says that soon after that, his house started becoming a mainstay for house shows in Gainesville. The band Utility only lasted for about a year and a half, but the Utility House remained for several years.

"All kinds of bands played there," Sweeting says. "Any band that was on tour in that era that wasn't big played at our house." From Los Crudos to Braid to KARP, the Utility House hosted them all.

Sweeting says he remembers those years as the heyday of the house show in Gainesville. "We would do a house show in like the '93, '94 era where we would draw like three or four hundred people....Where a club would do a show [featuring] Man or Astro-man? and get like one hundred people."

One house show in particular at that time would reverberate through the Gainesville scene for years in a very inconspicuous way. It was the summer of 1993, and the brutal, boundary-pushing New Jersey band Rorschach played with influential Florida grindcore band Assück at a house where scene regulars Jason Dooley and Drew Jackson lived.

Patrick Hughes remembers the show well; Rorschach's performance in particular that night blew him away. At the time, Rorschach was one of the most intense, aggressive bands in the punk world, with heavy yet technical guitar lines that churned behind the pained roar-scream of singer Charles Maggio.

"Here was this band that dodged all the late '80s and early '90s tough guy youth crew bullshit—they really took the intensity and they kept the

The Utility House in the mid-'90s. Bands represented here include Hot Water Music, Assholeparade, Palatka, Tired From Now On, Strikeforce Diablo, I Hate Myself, Gunmoll, Burnman, Pung, Highway 66, Ash County Sluggers, True North and Stressface. *Photograph by Matt Geiger.*

aggression. At the same time, they weren't like Green Day and these other bands," Hughes says.

Hughes was the independent music purchaser for Hyde and Zeke's at that point. After the show, with his glasses askew and "shaking and dripping with sweat," he approached Rorschach and asked them how he could get their music and other albums they were selling on tour into the store. They gave him the information for Ebullition Records in Goleta, California.

Ebullition Records and its mail-order distro, along with San Diego–based Gravity Records, would help fuel a whole new wave of post-hardcore bands in underground America in the 1990s. Bands like Still Life, Iconoclast and Heroin were mashing together influences from what were considered emo-core bands like Rites of Spring with more aggressive hardcore and sometimes metal bands. The result was an all-out emotional attack—the music was aggressive and angry, often with violent bursts of energy, yet it was not characterized by the testosterone-fueled baggage that usually accompanied aggressive music.

Hyde and Zeke's took a pass on Hughes's pitch to order from Ebullition. They were not interested in being on the cutting edge of the DIY underground. They had good, long-standing relationships ordering from places like SST and plenty of customers still coming in to buy that stuff.

But Hughes could see that the punk scene was in transition once again, as he had seen several times since the early 1980s. He was also personally searching for new inspiration. "Jon Resh moving away was kind of traumatic for me—the end of Spoke, and Scott going to Japan," Hughes says. "That really sucked to see that era pass."

Hughes decided to open his own record store with the help of his friend Mike Wohlgemuth. He would be able to carry any and all the punk and underground music he wanted to. The small store on University Avenue was called Shaft. Hughes stocked the place with the punk and hardcore basics like Bad Brains and Minor Threat, but he also stocked new and interesting records associated with Ebullition, bands like Integrity, and vegan straightedge bands that were popular at the time like Earth Crisis.

"I was like, something is happening here," Hughes says. "I felt like there was a resurgence happening and I wanted to be part of it and I lucked out....I remember the first day [of business] looking around like, 'Jesus Christ, I sold everything in the fucking store....I've got to get on the horn, I've got to get more stuff.' So something was really happening."

Shaft quickly became the go-to record store for punk and underground fans in Gainesville, of which there was a growing number. Hughes was a huge champion of the underground and was friends or acquaintances with just about every band in town.

Like Hughes, Matt Sweeting recognized Rorschach as a band that stood above their peers, exploring new territory. Sweeting had always gravitated toward heavy and aggressive music, and seeing Rorschach helped to crystallize some ideas about what he wanted to do with a band. That night he talked to Jason Dooley about forming a heavier band that would draw some influences from Rorschach, among others. The idea would eventually turn into Tired From Now On, a progressive, heavy, post-hardcore group that introduced a new element of heaviness to the Gainesville punk scene at the time. Tired From Now On's aggressive and cathartic approach was an intense emotional expression, with singer Major Jarman's guttural screams buried beneath a deluge of sludgy guitars and skidding time signatures.

The punk scene continued to diversify. Elsewhere in town, bands like Moonraker, led by Travis Fristoe, were marrying poetry, loud-soft dynamics and open-nerve honesty into a truly innovative package, not unlike some

Tired From Now On performing at the Club Downunder in Tallahassee. *Photograph by Wendy Mays.*

of the Ebullition or Gravity bands on the other side of the country. Fristoe had also fallen into the Gainesville punk scene during the Spoke and Radon era, even helping package the first Spoke seven-inch in Thelin's living room when it was initially pressed.

Fristoe, who came off as quiet and thoughtful during conversation, had the heart of a poet and the fierce spirit of an activist. In Moonraker and his subsequent bands, Reactionary 3 and True Feedback Story, and his long-running 'zine, *America?*, Fristoe combined those driving forces to create a singular spark. Though his bands never rose to the level of notoriety as some of the other bands Fristoe shared shows with in Gainesville, like the old legend about the Velvet Underground, his music made a lasting impression on those who experienced it.

By 1994, No Idea had released a series of seven-inches that captured the punk zeitgeist sweeping through Gainesville. In addition to Spoke, Radon and Less Than Jake, records by King Friday, When Puberty Strikes, Bombshell, Clairmel, Pung and more all serve as documents of Gainesville's

Vanbuilderass performing at the Hardback. *Photograph by Matt Geiger.*

early '90s scene. Thelin had also put out several records from non-Florida bands, including a split seven-inch by Jawbreaker and Samiam, which would both go on to wield great influence in the punk underground. Just a few years after Spoke's spark of momentum, No Idea had nearly thirty successful releases in its catalogue. (In the world of underground punk in those days, pressing five hundred or one thousand records at a time and getting rid of more than half of them was a success.)

For the last four years, Thelin had been working full time at a screen-printing shop in town and was doing No Idea Records on the side. A question that he had floating around in his head for years was, "What would you do if you had $10,000?" It even popped up in band interviews in the *No Idea* 'zine. (Ian MacKaye of Fugazi, ever the sensible businessman, replied in a 1989 interview that he does have $10,000.)

Thelin realized in 1994 that *he* now had $10,000 saved in his bank account as well. He had to answer to himself. "I was like, what does this mean? Does this mean I'm full of shit if I don't quit my job and try to do this?" Thelin says.

He made the leap, quitting his job and putting his money into turning No Idea (which was still run from his house) into a full-time record label. In the interim, he would also work with Hughes part time at Shaft, processing early No Idea mail orders behind the counter.

## 11.

# THE SOUND ENGINEER

An abundance of bands, a growing local punk label and an anything-goes punk venue were all major factors contributing to Gainesville's early '90s punk explosion. But another huge piece of the puzzle fell into place when The Hardback sound engineer Rob McGregor took up recording music—at first out of necessity, though it quickly turned into a passion and a profession.

"Recording was just a hobby so I wouldn't forget my songs," McGregor says. He would record his music to a tabletop cassette deck, then play the tape back through a boombox. Then he would play or sing again into the tabletop deck, which was also recording the playback from the boombox. Repeat until finished.

McGregor slowly made jumps in fidelity as he moved in with a roommate who had a stereo that allowed him to add tracks without having to play back through a separate boombox. He then eventually got an actual four-track cassette recorder. "Friends and bands I was in started wanting me to record them at this point. I really enjoyed helping people with their art and music and would do it pro bono for anyone who wanted me to help," McGregor says.

It just so happened that McGregor—himself a musician, a punk fan and the sound guy at The Hardback—knew just about every punk band in town and quickly became the go-to source for most of the punk-related recordings in Gainesville at the time and for years to come.

The bands no longer had to travel to Tallahassee to record with Tommy Hamilton or fork out bigger bucks to record in town at Mirror Image. Instead, they could just head down the road to McGregor's studio on Main Street, which was actually just the attic bedroom where McGregor lived at the time.

McGregor's first pro setup came when he was kidnapped by two local punk fans and supporters known as Jesus Gene and John the Baptist. McGregor says Jesus Gene was a fan of his tapes and wanted to help him further his recording career. They took him to Tampa and helped McGregor buy an eight-track digital tape recorder, a small mixing board, some mics, instrument cables, connectors, a headphone amp and headphones.

McGregor's first real studio setup was a partnership with Jesus Gene called Turd Studios (at Jesus Gene's request). When Jesus Gene moved to Orlando, McGregor decided it might sound a little more professional to change the name to Goldentone Studio, which he still uses to this day.

# 12.

# FINDING THE RHYTHMS

There were still ever-increasing numbers of punk fans moving to Gainesville. Many were drawn to town because of the usual ties to the University of Florida. But, more frequently than ever, it seemed that kids were moving to town because of the punk scene and No Idea Records.

At Shaft, Patrick Hughes was stocking the deepest and broadest selection of underground music in town and saw most of the punk scene come through his doors. At some point in the store's early days, a new band in town started hanging around. Sometimes they would linger for hours, just goofing off and talking about music. They gave Hughes a demo tape and would invite him to their shows, but he politely declined. He liked the guys and was afraid he'd be put in an awkward position because he didn't think he would like their music. Although they bought some records Hughes could get on board with, like Fugazi or Quicksand, he assumed they were a funk metal band, which was popular at the time, since they would wear Living Color or Fishbone T-shirts. They called themselves Hot Water Music.

The members of Hot Water Music had grown up around Sarasota, Florida, near Tampa—almost three hours south of Gainesville. Chris Wollard remembers being a young punk fan excited about area bands like No Fraud and People's Court and always looking for more new music.

"Then all of a sudden the Spoke seven-inch and the Radon seven-inch were at Daddy Kool Records…and you're like, what is this?!" Wollard says in an interview with the podcast Rocket Fuel. "And you're like, this—this is out of Florida, what the fuck? And you're like, Gainesville, Florida, where's that?…There's a label?"

Wollard was immediately intrigued by the bands and the scene he discovered coming out of Gainesville. When he saw that Spoke was playing a show at the New College in Tampa, he was there. Before long, Wollard and friends visited Gainesville and the SpokeHouse, with its flurry of activity. "I'd never seen a punk house before and it was like, ok, I'm moving here," Wollard says. Although Tampa had tons of punk shows and an active scene, Wollard says it lacked the unique neighborhood vibe of the Gainesville scene.

In 1993, Wollard was playing guitar in a punk band called Thread with his friends Jason Black on bass and George Rebelo on drums. Black and Rebelo had already been playing together for several years at that point, having met in the school jazz band. Rebelo was also playing drums in a grungy, metal-leaning group called Fossil with a guitar player named Chuck Ragan.

Ragan had also gotten wind of the Gainesville scene by that point. "It always seemed like something was going on [in Gainesville]. It always seemed like people were putting out records and there were shows and house shows every night, and you name it—just craziness," Ragan says.

When Black moved to Gainesville to attend UF, it was easy for Thread and Fossil to decide to relocate to Gainesville the following year. Wollard, Black and Ragan were already fans of the scene, and Rebelo, more of a metal head than punk fan, was up for the adventure, even though he says he wasn't even sure where Gainesville was at the time.

It wasn't long before Ragan, Wollard, Black and Rebelo were all living in Treehouse Village apartments in Gainesville. The singers from Thread and Fossil decided to stay behind in Sarasota and planned to commute to Gainesville to practice. As it happened, the singers never came to Gainesville and faded out of the picture pretty quickly, but the new Gainesville transplants were still practicing as if each band would continue.

"We all just ended up sitting on the porches at Treehouse Village," Ragan says. "And we couldn't really plug in amps there so we all started just writing songs on acoustic and terrorizing our little apartment complex and just working to keep paying the rent and put a little food in the fridge."

One day Wollard, Rebelo and Black were playing a song they had written for the now basically defunct Thread, and Ragan just started singing over it. The song would become "Us & Chuck," which would eventually appear on the band's first seven-inch. Those unofficial practices continued, and by the time they wrote their fourth or fifth song together in October 1994, the four musicians realized it was time to just officially become a band. After agonizing over a name, they decided on Hot Water Music—Wollard was reading the Charles Bukowski short story collection at the time, and they took their new name right off the cover.

Though they were fans of the Gainesville scene, the guys in Hot Water Music didn't really know many people in town very well and for the most part kept to themselves. They were hungry to play music and get involved, but the Gainesville scene didn't prove very welcoming in the beginning.

"They fucking hated us," Rebelo says.

The band's very first show was for a Jewish fraternity social at Durty Nelly's, a dimly lit Irish pub in downtown Gainesville. A friend of Black's from Sarasota was in the fraternity and was in desperate need of a band for the event. The crowd was mostly indifferent to the weird punk kids playing in the corner, until Hot Water Music played the only cover song they knew: Bryan Adams's "Summer of '69."

Hot Water got a little closer to reaching their desired audience when they played their second show at The Hardback with local hardcore bands Fried Christ and Section 8. But it would still be a while before they were accepted

Chris Wollard screams during an early Hot Water Music show at The Hardback. *Photograph by Matt Geiger.*

and, eventually, embraced by the scene. Like Less Than Jake, Hot Water Music was ambitious—and not shy about it. They practiced five times a week and played any time and any place they could in the early days.

"Looking back on it now, we definitely had to earn it because we weren't playing the kind of music that a lot of people were way into," Ragan says. "But man, I mean we just put everything we had into it and we loved it, and we could care less whether people liked it or not. It almost seemed like the more people that didn't like it, it kind of added more fuel to the fire."

Perhaps feeling a kinship in being the underdog, Chris DeMakes from Less Than Jake was the first person in town to show up to one of Hot Water Music's practices, to offer his support. And after Patrick Hughes finally saw the band play live, he and Tired From Now On drummer Jason Dooley quickly became big early supporters, defending the young band against naysayers in the scene.

Hughes, lacking the emotional connection to a band like he had with Spoke, was searching for something new to get behind when Hot Water came along.

"Hot Water Music, they were incendiary when they started out," Hughes says. "They would end up at shows playing in front of four or five people literally bleeding in the wreckage of their instruments and their lives. I got to be friends with those dudes, and I had a front-row seat to all that stuff. They were just a fucking force of nature when they started out."

The band's unrelenting nature, combined with the fact that they really were great musicians who were doing something innovative and interesting at the time, eventually sank in. Soon, the balance of support began shifting in their favor.

Hot Water Music's sound wasn't quite like anything else around at the time. Wollard and Ragan played guitar and sang—often with dueling and intertwining vocal lines—and both singers yelped and screamed with a thick, gravel-throated yell with just the right amount of melody behind it. And with Rebelo on drums and Black on bass, they held down one of the tightest and most impressive rhythm sections in punk rock. But there was no cohesive plan about what they wanted to sound like. The four members were coming from four different directions; when writing songs, they would just keep putting out ideas until they settled on something they could all get behind.

"Chuck wanted to be Pegboy, Jason kind of wanted to be Fugazi, Chris wanted to be the Doughboys and I wanted to be heavy," Rebelo says. "It was literally four people's takes on what they wanted the band to be and it was fighting resistance until we got to something that all four of us would be like, 'All right, cool.'"

The result was a blend of punk-rooted post-hardcore bursting with energy and emotion that was its own unique sound. A lot of influences were in the mix, but a couple that rise to the top of Hot Water Music's early work are the Dischord Records–influenced San Francisco Bay Area band Fuel (not to be confused with the late '90s radio rock band) and Leatherface, a British punk band that mastered the combination of introspective lyrics, gruff vocals and undeniable melodies.

Once they found their footing and got their first shows at The Hardback, there was no stopping Hot Water Music, whether people liked it or not. Maybe not since the Doldrums had the energy of a Gainesville punk band's

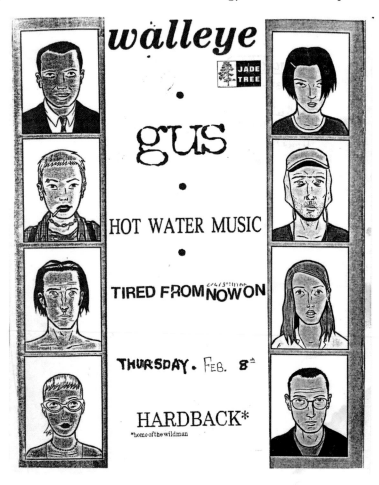

A flyer advertising a show featuring Delaware post-hardcore band Walleye, with Gus, Hot Water Music and Tired From Now On. *Courtesy of Matt Sweeting.*

live shows been as captivating. Hot Water Music's shows were an explosion of pent-up energy and emotion. Ragan and Wollard had big, bushy, unkempt beards at the time and would scream and lash around like wild men, completely uninhibited.

"We gave it a thousand percent every time," Rebelo says. "Our attitude was, we're not stopping for broken strings. There would be shows where Chris or Chuck would have like one string left. It probably didn't sound so good, but that was our attitude and kids responded to that....It was kind of a wild time."

"They played so much [in town] it was ridiculous," Matt Sweeting says. "You would see them like four or five times a month; they would play anywhere, anytime and absolutely go bananas, it was really cool. I feel really lucky to have gotten to see that....Chris has thrown his guitar through the wall and he's shirtless, and Chuck is bleeding, and George and Jason are just in the moment. That was their everything, it was awesome."

The band called it The Lifting.

"It was a reference for us that described our music and what it did for us, or the place or vision that it brought us either energetically or spiritually," Ragan said in a 2008 interview with *Satellite* magazine. "In short, it's a fully positive, exhilarating and uplifting experience through music on your own or with loved ones."

By May 1995, Hot Water Music had self-released *Push for Coin*, their first tape, and *Eating the Filler*, a seven-inch co-released by Hughes's Kung Fu Zombie record label and Toybox Records, another small local label run by Sean Bonner.

The band was preparing for their first tour that same year when, "after months of apprehension," they talked to Var Thelin about the prospect of releasing music on No Idea. The result of that meeting was *Finding the Rhythms*, a full-length CD of their first recordings that had been included on various seven-inches and compilation albums over the past year.

Once the band started touring, the road became their life. They shoved off in a cramped Chevy Astro van they named Black Lung and took their music to the rest of the country. Although at the time the straightedge and vegan movements didn't have a strong influence on the Gainesville scene, straightedge vegan hardcore bands were a big component of the larger punk underground scene, and Hot Water Music was a far cry from being vegan or straightedge.

"What people outside of Gainesville wanted was Hot Water Music to be a straightedge vegan band, and they weren't," Thelin says. "There was

Hot Water Music performing at The Hardback. This photograph was used in the Hot Water Music/Clairmel split release on No Idea. *Photograph by Matt Geiger.*

definitely a time when a band entered town and you're like, 'Wait, you're not a vegetarian?…I'm used to accommodating [vegetarians] and now you just want burgers?…You're eating burgers and getting drunk, oh weird.'"

As Hot Water Music took their explosive and emotional post-hardcore to the rest of America, more and more people began to become aware of Gainesville as a punk rock town.

# 13.

# LESS THAN JAKE GOES NATIONAL

It was during this time that Less Than Jake would quickly pick up momentum and go from a local act to a full-fledged national act. The band had become a fixture in the Gainesville scene by 1995. As their early seven-inches and compilation tracks filtered through the underground and their core audience grew, they caught the attention of Mike Park of the ska band Skankin' Pickle, who also had a small label called Dill Records. Park released a cassette demo with songs from his band and Less Than Jake, and the band agreed to put out their first full-length album, *Pezcore*, on Dill Records.

Less Than Jake were gearing up for their first "big" tour—a six-week jaunt across the country, playing mostly houses, basements, backyards and tiny venues. While booking the tour, the group had sent out copies of their self-released tape *Better Class of Losers*. Included in the tape was an early indication of drummer Vinnie Fiorello's and bassist Roger Lima's obsession with Pez dispensers. The inside note reads: "If you want lyrics, or feel the need to send Pez, write to…"; one side of the label reads, "Send," and the other reads, "Pez."

While *Pezcore* wasn't yet released when they hit the road, the album would arrive while they were in Chicago (the first time Less Than Jake were on a CD instead of vinyl or tape). The show was cancelled because of a citywide blackout, but they were able to sell copies of their new CD out of the back of their van to the fans who showed up.

Less Than Jake kicked off that tour with a show at The Hardback, and the band was surprised to learn that a representative from major-label giant

Capitol Records had flown in to watch the band play. Trombone player Buddy Schaub said an intern had gotten ahold of the Dill cassette demo with their songs on it and put the band on Capitol's radar.

The label rep turned up at shows a couple more times throughout the tour, and Less Than Jake eventually decided to sign to Capitol. Schaub says there was some blowback at the time from the underground community, who were very wary of major labels.

> *We'd always defend it just by being like, "Look, we write all the songs, we always had 100 percent creative control. We're doing what we want to do, we book our tours, we do it the way we want to do it." And at the end of the day if you can look at yourself and what you're doing with your life... and you're happy with how things are going and you're happy with all the decisions you've made for yourself...what everyone else says around you* [doesn't matter].

The group, with the addition of saxophonist Derron Nuhfer and the support of Capitol Records, released their major-label debut, *Losing Streak*, in 1996. The group went from backyards and basements to big stages in packed venues. The band's single, "Automatic," was getting airplay on MTV, and the album would break into the Top 20 on Billboard's Heatseekers chart. Throughout the following year, Less Than Jake toured with punk legends the Descendents and soon-to-be superstars Blink-182 and joined the fledgling punk festival the Warped Tour.

Throughout the frenzy of activity, Fiorello also found the time to establish a new record label in Gainesville, Fueled by Ramen, with co-founder John Janick. The label would initially be an outlet for various releases by Less Than Jake and like-minded ska and punk bands like The Hippos and The Impossibles.

# 14.

# GAINESVILLE PUNK DIVERSIFIES AND INNOVATES

During Hot Water Music's early years, while they were finding their sound and being rebuffed and eventually accepted by the Gainesville scene, and Less Than Jake was quickly on the rise, more diverse punk-influenced bands were cropping up in Gainesville. Some grew from seeds planted during Spoke and Radon's heyday, and others found inspiration in other trends flowing through the underground (and in some cases helped to set trends). Unlike earlier eras, there was not a singular overarching sound or pocket of influence that drove the Gainesville punk scene. Although Hot Water Music's post-hardcore blend would become known as the "Gainesville sound" to those outside the town, in Gainesville, punk was splitting in different directions.

Forming just on the heels of Hot Water Music in December 1994, a new band called Palatka occupied a drastically different space in the punk landscape. As Hot Water Music's popularity rose, they naturally progressed to larger stages, better-quality recordings and more accessible songs. Palatka, on the other hand, refused to play on stages at all or even mic their amplifiers. Their every move was intentional—acting almost as an anti-band in the Gainesville scene, eschewing any notion of what a punk band should be.

Singer Kurt Burja had been in Gainesville since 1991 and had been a big supporter of Radon and the other early Hardback bands. He had even released a live Radon album, though only a small number were sold, because many of them came back warped from the record pressing plant. But when Burja was ready to form his own band, he wanted a drastically different

Palatka performing at the Club Downunder in Tallahassee. *Courtesy of Mark Rodriguez.*

sound and approach than the quirky and melodic punk that had come to define the Gainesville scene.

Burja rounded up his friend Mike Taylor to play guitar and sing, Jason Teisinger to play bass and Mark Rodriguez to play drums. Palatka's music was informed by the lightning-fast hardcore bands of earlier days and captured the spirit of bands associated with San Diego's Gravity Records, like Heroin, Antioch Arrow, Mohinder and Angel Hair, fusing raw emotion with full-on chaotic aural assaults. Palatka's sound was characterized by singer Burja's unbridled terror-scream and short, noisy explosions of drums, guitar and bass.

Rodriguez says it seemed that Burja had the sound he wanted in his head from the beginning. Rodriguez, who was well versed in hardcore, pop punk and other underground music, wasn't quite sure what to think at first. In early practices he remembers Burja stopping him in mid-drumming. "I just want you to do this—like, just hit things," Burja would tell him. "I'm like, all right that seems weird, but ok," Rodriguez says.

But it didn't take long for the band members' personalities and musical styles to gel. After recording a tape that was much slower than the rest of their catalogue would be, they fell into their distinct chaotic blend of hardcore by the time they released a split seven-inch with Tampa band The

End of the Century Party. They soon added a second guitar player named Ryan Murphy to the lineup. Murphy had moved to town for college but says he had his sights set on living in Gainesville ever since he was blown away by a Moonraker show in his hometown of Daytona a couple of years earlier.

Palatka's lyrics, and the band itself, were pointedly political and even provocative at times, with songs tackling topics ranging from hardcore scene politics to broader social critiques about American culture and human rights. Some of the members of Palatka could be provocative within the Gainesville scene, as well. While other punk bands in Gainesville were always up for a party and lots of beer, Palatka had a more serious outlook and would call out other bands and punk fans for not thinking similarly.

Taylor says at the time he felt that, coming from a fairly privileged background, if one had a platform, "it's a waste of time to not discuss where you're from, what's good and bad about your city, how it interconnects with the national landscape, commonalities and differences."

"We were really, really harsh on everybody. People that just wanted to have a good time before finals," Taylor says. "Good people that liked to get loose, not feel like they had to be policed on every word they said.... Whenever people complain about Palatka being the PC police or whatever, it's my fault....Now I know you can speak your mind and express your values and still let people relate to music in their own way."

Palatka's pointed songs usually clocked in at under a minute long, and their whole set was often less than five minutes long. Such a short set was unusual, but the only time it caused a problem was when they played a club in Canada. After their five-minute set, the angry owner said they were supposed to play for thirty minutes. The best they could offer was to blow through the short set one more time.

The band's home base in Gainesville was the ironically named Megarock Arena, a punk house in the student ghetto with a tiny shed in the yard where they held shows. Palatka played and hosted many shows at Megarock, but they also played at The Hardback and the Utility House, among other places. Like Hot Water Music, they toured often, taking their cathartic, explosive sets across the country and into Canada and Europe.

By the mid-'90s, it was becoming increasingly common for any band to hit the underground tour circuit. The circuit had been evolving since the early '80s, when bands like Minor Threat and Black Flag were laying its foundations based on their tireless DIY efforts and building connections with kids and clubs throughout the country. In 1992, punk 'zine *Maximum Rocknroll* released the first edition of *Book Your Own Fuckin' Life*, a handy

A flyer advertising a show at the Cuban Embassy with Columbia, South Carolina's In/
Humanity and Gainesville's Palatka, Section 8 and Pung. *Courtesy of Mark Rodriguez.*

directory that compiled information about punk venues, bands and houses across the country. While booking a tour was still an incredible feat in the age of landline phones, long-distance phone cards and handwritten letters, the guide made it easier than it had ever been. By the mid-'90s, the guide had filtered down throughout the punk community, resulting in a marked increase of punk bands traveling across the country.

Between booking shows, touring and recording, Palatka quickly found a kinship in bands like The End of the Century Party and South Carolina's In/Humanity. A subgenre name even sprung up around Palatka and their peers: emoviolence. The term was a joke that originated with In/Humanity, based on the rampant naming of punk subgenres of the time; it combined the increasingly maligned "emo" descriptor with the similarly mocked "powerviolence." Although it was meant as a joke, the term lingered and remains associated with those bands.

It wasn't long after Palatka found their footing that another brutal hardcore band popped up in town, called Assholeparade. Formed by members of earlier hardcore bands Section 8 and Fried Christ, Assholeparade drew from some of the same early hardcore influences as Palatka but leaned toward a more singular and aggressive style. The faster, the better.

Travis Ginn and Travis Johnson grew up skateboarding together in nearby St. Augustine and moved to Gainesville together in late 1993. They were both fans of loud, aggressive, fast music and knew of Gainesville's vibrant punk scene. But once they got to town, it wasn't quite what they'd hoped for.

"I think we were both a little bummed when we moved to town," says Johnson. "All the local bands it seemed were like, pop punk." Johnson says it didn't take long for him to be swayed, though. "Jawbreaker and Crimpshrine, they just weren't bands I gave a shit about when I moved there, and within a year or two, I just lived by that shit."

Shortly after arriving in Gainesville, Ginn and Johnson had formed Fried Christ with Jamie Spall and Gainesville native Shane Haven. The group stayed active for about a year, playing fast, '80s-style hardcore. Haven and Johnson remember Hot Water Music opening for Fried Christ at that Hardback show. Ginn, who made the flyer for the show, drew Hot Water Music's name in tiny letters at the very bottom corner of the flyer.

"I remember we thought they were going to be a terrible bluegrass band or something with that name," Haven says. "But they killed it, and we all became immediate friends that night."

"They started playing and me and Shane were like, holy shit," Johnson says. "It was like, oh yeah, these guys aren't fucking around, they are nailing it."

Fried Christ eventually fizzled out, but Ginn was still determined to play fast hardcore. He regrouped with Brian Johnson of Section 8 on guitar, Chris Campisi of Highway 66 on bass and Jon Weisberg of Vanbuilderass on drums to form Assholeparade. The band's mission was basically to play fast and brutal and to party all along the way.

Though there were overlapping musical characteristics, Assholeparade was less political than Palatka; Ginn was more likely to scream about skateboarding for forty-five seconds than about progressive political ideals. There was a natural tension based on the two bands' opposite approaches, but the groups shared a practice space and frequently played shows together. In the meantime, Johnson had formed Ansojuan with friends from St. Augustine, but it wasn't long before he replaced Campisi on bass and Assholeparade began touring, taking their "fastcore" across the country.

Assholeparade performing at the final night of The Hardback. *Photograph by Mike Collins.*

Ash County Sluggers performing at The Hardback. *Photograph by Matt Geiger.*

Campisi continued on, playing bass with a new band called Ash County Sluggers. Brent Wilson, who had moved to Miami at the end of Radon's most active period, moved back to town in 1995 and started Ash County Sluggers shortly thereafter, with Campisi, his old bandmate Bill Clower and Randy Brownell, who had played guitar in Don's Ex-Girlfriend.

Assholeparade eventually sought a second guitarist after going into the studio with Rob McGregor. McGregor made Brian Johnson record two guitar tracks for each song, and they realized how much fuller they sounded with double guitars. They soon brought Drew DeMaio of Gus and Strikeforce Diablo into the mix for a while. He was then replaced by Chuck Ragan for one practice, and the group finally settled in with Matt Sweeting from Tired From Now On and, also by that point, Strikeforce Diablo.

If Assholeparade represented the fastest sect of the Gainesville punk scene, I Hate Myself represented the slowest—though their songs could be equally heavy in their own way, carrying their weight in a different distribution.

Like many punk fans who would go on to form bands in Gainesville, Jim and Jon Marburger's first exposure to punk rock came when Jim brought home the Spoke and Radon seven-inches one day, borrowed from a high school friend. The brothers had moved to Gainesville in the late '80s when they were in elementary school and were big music fans. But up to that point, they had little exposure to underground music. Pretty soon, Jim's friend Aaron Martin began giving them mixtapes with a broader view of the punk and underground rock world, with bands like Mission of Burma, Big Black and the Pixies.

The brothers, with Jim singing and playing guitar, Jon on drums and Martin on bass, soon formed their first punk band, Pung (the band Patrick Hughes would later terrorize with Black Cats), right at the tail end of the Spoke era. Still in high school, the brothers played their first Pung show at The Hardback to a nearly empty room. After their set, a tall, lanky mustached punk rocker introduced himself to them as Danarchy. "Hey, you guys are young, you'll get better. It was fun," he said. Jon says Danarchy was very supportive of Pung and the Marburger brothers from the very beginning, helping to make them feel comfortable in a world that was new to them.

Danarchy was a Hardback fixture and one of the punk scene's biggest supporters. He began hanging out at the club as soon as it opened and started working there not long after. He's known for the giant tattoo of

The Hardback Café across his back and the graveyard of names of defunct Gainesville punk bands tattooed on his chest. During the '90s, Danarchy could be found at The Hardback nearly every night.

And Pung did get better. They were a fairly straightforward punk band and perhaps the most conventional band the Marburger brothers would play in, but there were clues even then that they would want to explore new territory outside of a standard three-chord punk progression. Var Thelin was a fan, releasing their *Danarchy* seven-inch on No Idea not long after the band began. Thelin would also later join the band when Martin left to focus on school.

After Pung had run its course, Jim and Jon began toying with a new project called I Hate Myself, born out of a Pung song that was much slower than the rest of their catalogue. Originally a four-piece including Ryan Murphy of Palatka and Jason Dooley of Tired From Now On, the band quickly evolved into a three-piece with Jon Marburger on drums, Jim Marburger on guitar and vocals and Steve Parsley on bass.

Musically, I Hate Myself relied on being very slow and deliberate, with sharp contrasts between quiet, almost meditative segments that rip into loud and heavy portions driven by Jim Marburger's tidal-wave scream. Jim says he discovered his powerful scream almost by accident one day while singing along to an Assfactor 4 seven-inch. He was also inspired at the time by Ebullition bands like Julia and Still Life.

Though the brothers took the music and the band seriously, there was a subtle irony to the whole thing from the very beginning. Jim was aware that he was leaning toward the saccharine side of expression with some of I Hate Myself's sad-sack lyrics. Although they seemed very serious about the whole ordeal, it was always a little bit tongue-in-cheek. Even the name was something Jim told Patrick Hughes as a joke.

"That was absolutely the deal from the get-go with I Hate Myself," Hughes says. "Jim mocking his own emo tendencies and the genre while simultaneously indulging and celebrating both."

In playing up those emo tendencies and consciously pursuing overt expressions of sadness, Jim's lyrics ranged from obviously jokey to genuine poetry that at times hearkened back to Moonraker and Travis Fristoe's vivid and moody lyrics.

The Marburgers say that I Hate Myself was met with little fanfare in Gainesville at the time. But the band's catalogue would eventually filter into the evolving world of underground emo and post-hardcore and become highly influential in the continuum of those genres. Like the term "emoviolence" for Palatka, I Hate Myself would become known as a cornerstone of the "screamo" genre.

The AV Club calls I Hate Myself "one of screamo's most important acts" and the song "To a Husband at War" from their album *10 Songs* "a high-water mark for the genre." They have often been included on "best-of" lists, including *OC Weekly*'s "Top 10 Emo Bands of the '90s," just behind Jawbreaker and Sunny Day Real Estate.

# 15.

# BREAKING UP, REGROUPING

The mid-1990s was obviously a boom period for Gainesville punk rock. It was also a time of expansion for No Idea Records, as Thelin embraced its status as a legitimate record label and began to shed its origins as a punk fanzine. Thelin's label had become synonymous with Gainesville punk, and now that Less Than Jake and Hot Water Music were carrying their music across the country in a way bigger than any Gainesville punk band had before, No Idea's name was spreading, as well.

Thelin even expanded the label to include a mail-order record distribution business. After a brief partnership under the name Blindspot, with Sean Bonner, who ran Toybox Records at the time, the No Idea distro was established, allowing the label to position itself as not only a "Gainesville record label" but also a place to turn for a much broader selection of punk records.

It wasn't long before Thelin would be bringing on part-time and then full-time employees at No Idea, including Jon Marburger of I Hate Myself and Matt Sweeting of Tired From Now On and Assholeparade. Thelin also met his future wife around this time, Jennifer Crosby, whom he credits with keeping the label alive. "She moved up [to Gainesville] and realized a disaster was looming," Thelin told *Razorcake* magazine in 2010. "She single-handedly beat back the wolves and straightened out the nightmare. We started getting paid for the records we shipped. What a revolutionary idea!…Without Jennifer, not only would I be a hopeless mess living under someone's couch, there would be no No Idea as we know it."

Despite the flourishing punk scene and No Idea's expansion, things weren't looking as good for Alan Bushnell and The Hardback. Even though the punks showed up every night, the business itself was struggling. Bushnell also had aspirations to run for public office and even go to law school to become a public defender. He had also been living in a homemade apartment in the back of The Hardback since 1992, following his divorce.

"I had a kid, I started thinking about the future," Bushnell says. "It was getting hard to pay the bills for a while, and I felt, 'Well, maybe people just perceive that it's a punk rock club and they're scared to come here.'"

So, Bushnell closed down The Hardback and, in an attempt to draw a broader crowd, reopened it as the Lyric, a 1990s coffeehouse that held poetry readings but rarely hosted full-band shows. The new business didn't go over well with the punks or with the town in general; by early 1997, Bushnell was ready to be out of it for good. Drew DeMaio asked him on a whim how much he would sell the business for. Bushnell said $5,000.

DeMaio, who had moved to Gainesville from South Florida with his band Gus (which at the time included drummer Sam Fogarino, who would go on to play drums in popular indie rock band Interpol), went back to the Utility House with the proposal, where he was living with Matt Sweeting and others. Sweeting said he rounded up the money and brought it to Bushnell the very next day.

The Hardback returned soon afterward, this time with Sweeting and DeMaio at the helm.


Hot Water Music released their first full-length album, *Fuel for the Hate Game*, with No Idea and Toybox Records in 1997. *Fuel* found Hot Water Music refining their sound from their earlier seven-inches, dialing in the push-pull of Ragan's and Wollard's dueling vocals and ramping up the energy. They were still going full-bore on the tour circuit, playing houses and tiny clubs all over the country and pushing themselves to exhaustion.

"That's our time, that's our space, that's our outlet to release, so we do everything we can to get it all out at the time," Chuck Ragan told Todd Taylor in a 1999 interview for the California punk 'zine *Flipside*. "By the end, you're fucking spent."

Chris Wollard told Taylor he would often vomit after the shows. "Sometimes you're just so worked up. All of a sudden it's over and your body can't even handle that. You're just sitting there, and sometimes it's really hard to wind down."

Amid touring and playing shows back home, Hot Water found the time to write their next record, *Forever and Counting*. Instead of releasing the album on No Idea, the band decided to partner with Ohio's Doghouse Records because the label would be able to help the band tour Europe for the first time. But despite all the time they had spent on the road in the United States, the European tour essentially broke Hot Water Music. Not knowing the different cultures they were immersed in, trying to figure out exchange rates in the pre-Euro currency days and generally feeling isolated led to the bandmates fighting constantly and pushing their friendships to the limits.

"We didn't have any money and we were surrounded by all these people we couldn't talk to, so we were miserable and taking it out on each other like brothers, fighting all the time," Wollard said in an interview with *Alternative Press*. In an attempt to salvage their friendships, the band decided that, after the tour, they would call it quits. When Hot Water Music got home to Gainesville, they put away their instruments and went their separate ways.

After a few weeks, tensions faded a bit, and the band members started hanging out again as friends. Someone had the idea that Hot Water Music should play one final show at The Hardback, and Thelin had the idea to record the show and release it as a live album. The members of the band met up at Happy Hour Pool Hall before the show, and the idea was thrown around that maybe Hot Water Music should carry on, though, according to Rebelo, they never came to a conclusion before the show started.

Later that night, The Hardback was packed beyond capacity. Friends that Hot Water Music had made on the road and fans coming from all over the country and as far away as Germany and Japan were jammed into the tiny club and spilling out into the streets and onto the neighboring steps of the Hippodrome Theatre.

"It was fucking insane," Rebelo says. "At that point in my life I had never seen anything like it."

After they played their first song, Wollard announced on the mic that the band had decided to stay together. The news was met with wild cheers and applause. For Rebelo, it wasn't until that show that he realized how much of an impact Hot Water Music had already made in their first few years as a band.

"I think for us, the reaction of the kids coming from around the world—and it doesn't seem like a lot, I guess—but to a punk rock kid in Gainesville playing at The Hardback, it meant everything to us," Rebelo says. "I don't know that I can do anything else with my life that will connect to people the way that made me feel, like holy shit, I don't even know these fucking people and they're here to support little old me and my band in Gainesville, Florida....What an opportunity it is to branch out to the world."

Hot Water Music's brief sabbatical reenergized them in a big way, and they came back stronger and hungrier than ever. By the end of 1999, they would release their leanest, most driving record to date, *No Division,* and continue life on the road, touring with just about every notable punk band of the day, including Leatherface, one of their biggest influences.

# 16.
# GAINESVILLE PUNK THRIVES

The late 1990s saw a whole new wave of bands springing up in Gainesville and even fully formed bands relocating to Gainesville. A Gainesville Hardcore Fest popped up in town for a couple of years, which was very loosely affiliated with the Gainesville punk scene but attracted some of the top punk, hardcore and emo bands of the day to play. While not as big as other independent labels like Fat Wreck Chords or Epitaph, No Idea Records was a firmly established and respected staple of the underground punk scene by then, much like Dischord in Washington, D.C., which No Idea was largely modeled after. Assholeparade and Palatka were still going strong, but I Hate Myself effectively came to an end after a short but prolific two-year run before evolving into Burnman. (Palatka would also call it quits just before the new millennium after releasing their final album, *The End of Irony*, on No Idea.) Even the members of Hot Water Music, in between their rigorous tour schedule, were starting side projects, like the softer-leaning Blacktop Cadence, Baroque, Unitas and the Americana-tinged Rumbleseat.

Leading the charge of anthemic, aggressive and catchy punk rock during that period was a new band called Panthro U.K. United 13 (a name unnecessarily long, meant as a satire of the lengthy emo and post-hardcore band names that were popping up at the time). The band comprised former members of Don's Ex-Girlfriend—Alex Ulloa on guitar and vocals and Jimmy Wysolmierski on bass—along with former Fried Christ drummer Shane Haven and former Don't Be One guitarist Bryan Yeager. The basis of Panthro's sound called

A flyer advertising a show at The Hardback featuring Richmond, Virginia's Avail and Gainesville's Hot Water Music, Discount and Panthro U.K. United 13. *Courtesy of Matt Sweeting.*

back to the catchier melodic punk of the early '90s Gainesville bands, with an aggressive edge drawing from '80s hardcore. Panthro was a staple of the late '90s Gainesville scene—their singalong choruses reverberating often through the walls of the tiny Hardback Café—before calling it a day in January 2000, as the members moved on to other projects.

Even catchier than Panthro was Discount, a pop-punk band formed in Vero Beach, Florida, in 1995 that moved north to Gainesville in 1998. The group was fronted by singer Alison Mosshart, at the time a short-haired, bouncy punk kid singing some of the most infectious melodies to ever come out of Florida. The group had a prolific output of seven-inch releases, split seven-inches, compilation tracks and three full-length albums. They quickly developed a strong following in Florida and were making waves in the punk underground across the country. They were hailed by some as one of the best punk bands to come out of Florida in the 1990s.

Hot Water Music often toured with both Discount and Panthro U.K. United 13, even taking Discount to Europe twice. Discount only lasted in Gainesville for about two years before breaking up in 2000. Mosshart went

Panthro U.K. United 13 performing at a house party. *Photograph by Matt Geiger*.

Discount, during their final show at the Market Street Pub in Gainesville. *Photograph by Karen Hodges*.

on to form The Kills, which would become an international success, and later joined the The Dead Weather with Jack White.

Another late '90s addition to the Gainesville scene was As Friends Rust. Singer Damien Moyal had fronted both Morning Again and Culture, two of the most active metal-influenced hardcore bands in South Florida that were also a big part of the vegan straightedge movement of the time. Culture relocated from Miami to Gainesville in 1997, essentially to be closer to the rest of the United States when they started out on their tours. After Culture dissolved fairly quickly in Gainesville, Moyal and some of his Culture bandmates decided to revive an earlier project of Moyal's called As Friends Rust.

As Friends Rust traded Culture's heavy chugga-chugga guitars for more expansive and diverse guitar work, and Moyal dialed back his throat-shredding screams to more melodic levels. Moyal and the other members also began diverging from the straightedge and vegan movements that had played a huge role in Culture's identity as a band. As Friends Rust dealt more in the personal than the political. Like Discount, As Friends Rust spent much of their time on the road during their most active four years as a band. Although they had a local following, they often drew bigger crowds outside

As Friends Rust performing at the Atlantic in Gainesville at their 2008 reunion show. *Photograph by Nicholas Forneris.*

of Gainesville, particularly in Europe, where Culture had developed a large fan base.

And there was Strikeforce Diablo, featuring Hardback co-owners Drew DeMaio singing and playing guitar and Matt Sweeting on bass and their friend Kevin Scott on drums. The band evolved from the ashes of DeMaio's previous band, Gus, which, like Culture, ended fairly quickly after the band moved from Miami to Gainesville. Strikeforce's rhythmic and dynamic guitar play pushed and pulled, building and releasing tensions with the rhythm section of Sweeting and Scott, as DeMaio's dramatic vocals would swing from melodic to a full-throated scream. In some ways, it brought together elements of everything Gainesville punk had accomplished up to that point. It was smart, heavy, catchy, energetic, full of passion and executed in true DIY fashion.

Bill Bryson, the owner of the Covered Dish, was also making music. He joined the high-concept, punk-influenced group The Causey Way in 1997 with founding This Bike Is a Pipe Bomb member Scott Stanton. The band toured often and never established a solid home base in Gainesville, but they were signed to Alternative Tentacles, which was owned by Dead Kennedys frontman Jello Biafra. It was a little bit of irony for the punks who didn't want to do business with Bryson.

As the decade came to a close, No More, a Port Charlotte pop punk band whose members were just a few years younger than Chris DeMakes and Vinnie Fiorello of Less Than Jake, also made the move to Gainesville. Singer and guitarist Jennifer Vito said Less Than Jake always tried to give back to the younger kids in the scene when they came through Port Charlotte and would invite No More to open shows for them. And when No More moved up to Gainesville, Less Than Jake showed them the ropes in town, helping them secure a practice space and a place to live.

Vito says she always felt No More was welcomed into the scene and made to feel a part of it almost immediately. She said she has memories of Sweeting and DeMaio from The Hardback, Chuck Ragan of Hot Water Music and the members of Crash Pad (a long-running Gainesville punk band fronted by Brian Kruger, who first played in The Atomics alongside Roach Motel) being very supportive in various ways. And, as a woman in the punk scene, Vito says local musicians like Samantha Jones, Jessica Mills and Margo Briggs were all very welcoming.

"I really didn't know any other girls that played music in my hometown, and when I moved here one of our first shows was at Kate's Fish Camp," Vito says. "And Samantha came up to me and was like, 'Hey, I want to

No More performing at the Civic Media Center. *Courtesy of Jennifer Vito.*

welcome you,' and introduced me to other ladies and they all at different points came up and were really encouraging and invited me to hang out."

Vito would also quickly join the local Radical Cheerleaders, an activist group that at the time was protesting against the FCC shutting down Free Radio Gainesville, a low-powered political radio station. One of their protest chants can be heard at the beginning of Hot Water Music's song "Free Radio Gainesville" on their album *No Division.*

Samantha Jones moved to Gainesville in the early '90s and has been a prolific musician in the scene. In the 1990s, she was involved in a plethora of musical projects, including Vanbuilderass, Baroque, Bitchin', Rumbleseat and the fondly remembered Lazy Slobs. She says the Gainesville punk scene has always had a strong female presence and has generally been supportive of women.

"There was a sense that there was a space for women to play. You didn't have to play in an all-girl band," Jones says. "I find that as a woman, people are surprised if I don't play folk music or punk music. If there's any dynamics or variation within that, it's always a huge surprise."

She says there were challenges over the years, though, like when she was playing a show with her longtime band Crustaceans.

*I was looking down at my tuner and on either side of my tuner these sneakers are there because some dude is standing that close to me, and I look up and he's nose to nose with me and he's like, "You can't play that bass." Fortunately, I had just tuned. The drummer counted off the song and we started with this super burly jam that was like a racehorse out the gate from the very first note. That guy apologized to me after we played.*

# 17.

# THE END OF AN ERA

It was late 1998, and Gainesville punk was charging forward stronger than ever, with several groups hitting the national scene and numerous bands filtering through and influencing the underground. By this time, just by being a "Gainesville band," a group was given a little extra attention in the underground.

Despite the rising national reputation, things were once again looking bad for The Hardback's future. Sweeting and DeMaio found out that they would have to close The Hardback for good. The building was so dilapidated that it would take a big investor to bring it up to working condition. It was quite literally held together by duct tape. Although Sweeting and DeMaio scraped together the $85,000 to purchase the building from Alan Bushnell's family, another buyer had swooped in in the meantime and made the deal. The new owner had plans to clean the place up and bring in a more wholesome business what would be more appealing to the Hippodrome and Sun Center crowds.

The final two shows at The Hardback were on January 14 and 15, 1999. Twenty-six bands performed over the two nights, playing three songs each.

"This is the end of a generation," Sweeting told the *Alligator*. "It feels very odd. Almost surreal. It's like throwing away your old tennis shoes. You know how it works."

The lineup of the final shows provides a clear record of the bands driving the Gainesville scene in those days, with a few welcome reunions. The mix of bands encompassed the breadth of what the Gainesville scene had

only 2 nights left. hardback cafe.

thursday jan. 14th **hot water music**  reina aveja  **discount crustations**  **habituals**  as friends rust  **keith welsh**  true feedback story  **le tigre**  standing tall  **cave inline**  no more  **most hated**

friday jan. 15th **strikeforce diablo**  radon  **panthro uk united 13**  **assholeparade**  **grain**  rumbleseat  **section 8**  palatka  **lexingtons**  brittle stars  **argentina**  young americans  **clearance clarence revolver**

2 days, 26 bands, 3 songs each. shows start at 10pm sharp. $3 (benefit for new space) hardback cafe 232 se 1st ave 352.372.6248 bands please be there by 9:30 or else.

*Left*: A flyer for the final two nights of shows at The Hardback Café. *Courtesy of Matt Sweeting.*

*Below*: Strikeforce Diablo performing as the final band on the last night of The Hardback Café. *Photograph by Matt Geiger.*

Danarchy fire-breathing on top of The Hardback during its final night.
*Photograph by Matt Geiger.*

become. Hot Water Music, Discount, True Feedback Story, As Friends Rust, Radon, Panthro U.K. United 13, Strikeforce Diablo, Assholeparade, Grain, Argentina and more shared the bill. They were all bands that sound drastically different yet share overlapping influences, values and passions. All Gainesville punk.

That final show was a sad celebration. Strikeforce Diablo was the last band to play, and it would be their last show for the foreseeable future. Sweeting,

A love note from the punks of Gainesville after the final Hardback show. *Courtesy of Matt Sweeting.*

DeMaio and Scott dressed in tuxedos, accented by red bow ties. Sweeting and DeMaio screamed at the top of their lungs as the crowd encircled them. It was the end, but it was a triumphant end.

The Hardback was dismantled that Friday night. Patrons tore the latticework from the ceiling, broke windows and smashed beer bottles against the walls. Danarchy, armed with a torch, breathed fire through a broken window panel, then took to the roof to blow a flame high into the night sky.

Eventually, Gainesville's riot police showed up to ensure that things didn't get too out of hand, but no arrests were made. It was ultimately a peaceful farewell. The punks weren't lashing out at anybody—they were just sending The Hardback off the only way they knew how.

Danarchy told the *Alligator*: "It can close after a night like this. This is the only way to close this place. If this hadn't had happened, I would've been disappointed. Let it burn down because I don't live here anymore."

It truly was the end of an era. The Hardback had seen the Gainesville punk scene evolve from its '80s punk roots to a thriving and diverse national influencer. Gainesville punk would once again retreat and evolve and soon produce perhaps its most celebrated and at times maligned band to date, Against Me!

## PART III
# REINVENTING, 2000–2006

# 18.

# GAINESVILLE PUNK DISPERSES

The Gainesville punk scene had come a long way since bands like Roach Motel and the Mutley Chix bounced around town, booking shows at community centers and dragging around rented PA systems. Between The Hardback, No Idea Records, Rob McGregor and countless talented bands, Gainesville was a thriving punk town. Yet, like punk rock in general, it still tended to fly under the radar in the overall community. No matter how popular, credible or influential Gainesville punk was to the national underground, in Gainesville there would always be more people lined up to see hometown radio rock act Sister Hazel than there would be to see Hot Water Music.

With The Hardback closing its doors for good in 1999, the Gainesville scene no longer had a central hub where members from most punk bands in town gathered to drink, exchange stories, start new bands and come up with new ideas. The Hardback also took with it its role as an incubator for bands, having nurtured groups like Spoke, Radon, Less Than Jake, Hot Water Music and many more, allowing them to evolve and thrive because of its anything-goes approach to live music. The scene would regroup and evolve and, over the course of the next few years, reinvent itself once more.

The Gainesville punk scene took the loss of The Hardback in stride. Luckily, there were already machinations in motion that would allow the scene to keep moving forward, Hardback or not. The tightknit scene was dispersed

Reactionary 3 performing at Wayward Council. *Photograph by Jeff McMullen.*

for a while as house shows increased and other venues in town began booking more shows, like Market Street Pub, Common Grounds and the Down-Lo.

The Ark, a warehouse and former UF-sponsored art space on the east side of town, also picked up some of the shows in The Hardback's absence. Mike Taylor of Palatka had moved into The Ark with a group of friends in 1999. The warehouse was used as a free space, and there were typically between five and seven people living there at any given time. People would cycle out as new people would move in every few years. The Ark residents tended to be more politically and socially minded than people in some other parts of the scene, encouraging art, activism and creativity and actively promoting diversity in a more conscious way.

Over the years, The Ark hosted some of Gainesville's biggest DIY shows and also facilitated the punk bands in town that weren't necessarily interested in playing clubs, like The Goddamn Deluge, Slang and Reactionary 3.

The Covered Dish also picked up some shows that might have been at The Hardback, but it closed its doors just a year after The Hardback. Owner Bill Bryson was on the road a lot with The Causey Way and says after almost a decade, he had somewhat checked out from the Covered Dish and was ready to move on. The Dish and the other venues helped as a stopgap, but there wasn't another central venue yet that shared the same DIY, punk rock mindset with the scene as The Hardback had.

Travis Ginn of Assholeparade was working at Market Street Pub at the time, located just a few blocks northwest of where The Hardback was in downtown, and began to book some of those shows that would have previously been at The Hardback.

"At first the owners were like, 'Do what you want,' and for a while the shows were a lot of fun," Ginn says. "Matt Sweeting and Tony Weinbender were helping me a lot with those shows by basically booking the whole show and then just letting it happen at Market Street, which was awesome. They were loosely run and a lot of fun."

Tony Weinbender had moved to Gainesville in January 2000 from Harrisonburg, Virginia, where he went to college. Weinbender had been booking shows in Virginia since the mid-'90s and had forged relationships with many Gainesville bands, including Hot Water Music and Less Than Jake. He had been integral in starting the annual Mid-Atlantic College Radio Conference in Harrisonburg. Weinbender also played saxophone in Swank, a Virginia punk staple of the 1990s that often played shows with Hot Water Music, Less Than Jake and Richmond's Avail.

Weinbender had toured with Less Than Jake a few times as their merch person, where he would also occasionally throw on ridiculous costumes and dance around as part of their stage show. During one of their tours, Fiorello brought up the prospect of Weinbender working at his Fueled by Ramen record label with Fiorello's business partner, John Janick. Weinbender was still in college at the time, but he dropped out for what seemed like a good opportunity at a growing record label. But when he moved to town, Gainesville didn't seem like the same town he had traveled to so many times for shows at The Hardback. Most of the Gainesville friends he made over the years were out touring more often than they were home, so he didn't know many people or have connections in town. But he was still known to punk bands on the touring circuit as a guy who could book shows, so he began getting calls from bands that wanted to play in Gainesville.

"Within the first month I lived here I got a call from Strike Anywhere and it was like, 'We want to come through on tour, you used to do shows in Virginia and you moved here—where do we do shows?'" Weinbender remembers. "I was like, fuck, I don't know."

Weinbender began scoping out possible show spaces around town. He walked into a business on University Avenue called Common Grounds and asked the owner, Nigel Hamm, if they ever booked shows there. Hamm told him they had had shows there occasionally in the past.

"It was originally a coffeehouse with craft beer, that kind of stuff, but not really a bar," Hamm says. "People were sitting around playing chess...and then ska bands needed a place to play and that's kind of how it went."

Weinbender booked the show with Strike Anywhere and As Friends Rust on the bill. He said about twenty people showed up, but it led to Weinbender booking more shows at Common Grounds. He then branched out to the Purple Porpoise near the college and began working with Ginn to book shows at Market Street.

"You'd walk in [to Market Street] and it was an ice chamber because Ginn would get in there in the middle of summer to work and he'd turn the AC down so low, it was freezing in there. But it was a great spot," Weinbender says.

Eventually, the shows at Market Street tapered off. "As with most good things, [the owners] saw that they could be making more money from the door and started asking me for more of this and that," Ginn says. "It got to the point that it just wasn't the same anymore."

More and more punk shows began happening at Common Grounds, though. Pretty soon, it flipped from being a coffeehouse to being an actual venue space, since Hamm and his staff were willing to change with the shifting tides in town.

"There was a huge vacuum, like where are we going to play?" says Jason Rockhill, who was Hot Water Music's tour manager at the time and would pick up shifts at Common Grounds between tours. "So it became a place where other people, other than the weird group of misfits that hung out at Common Grounds to begin with, wanted to start playing shows...it seems like by accident."

While the punk bands were shuffling through different venues and house shows, Matt Sweeting and friends Laura Predny, Don Fitzpatrick and Frank Barber were working on securing a location for a new venture—a volunteer-run record store and show space. Patrick Hughes had decided to close Shaft in 1998, in part due to finances, but he was also itching to broaden his worldview and pursue a degree at UF.

"I was just feeling like I had basically built up a very safe fortress for myself. I had built up this imaginary, fantasy little punk world, where all the information I got came from the liner notes of records and 'zines," Hughes says. "And I would spend hours on the phone talking to [Ebullition's] Kent McClard and Karin Gembus from Spitboy, who was my distributor at Mordam Records."

Frank Barber came up with the idea for the new venture as he and friends were mourning the loss of Shaft and their local source for punk, hardcore and indie music. They brought up the idea to open their own version of Shaft to Sweeting, who was quickly on board. They fleshed out the concept and came up with the name, Wayward Council.

"The original intention of Wayward was to make punk, hardcore and other independent records accessible to the community and at a reasonable cost," Predny told the *Satellite* magazine. "It was an alternative to the status quo and typical capitalistic consumer experience."

Sweeting had the idea to take on the project with no capital investment by operating Wayward Council out of The Hardback on Saturday mornings, using records provided by No Idea, where Sweeting also worked. The new Wayward Council crew would pull four hundred to five hundred records from No Idea each Friday night and put sticky notes with prices on them, then haul the merchandise over to The Hardback early Saturday mornings, when they would set up shop. They would then take the unsold records back to No Idea and pay them the cost of the records and keep the difference.

The Saturday-morning sales happened right up until The Hardback closed down, and then Wayward Council operated out of The Down-Lo while they evaluated pursuing a full-time space.

By 2001, the group had saved enough money to open a modest storefront on University Avenue, where they realized their vision of maintaining a "not-for-profit volunteer/collectively-run record store, all ages show and community space."

While The Hardback, with an assist from No Idea, gave birth to Wayward Council, the new volunteer-run space would pretty quickly take on an identity of its own. It would be less of a punk clubhouse and more of a political and community-minded free space. It appealed more to the activist-minded punks in town than to those looking for a booze-fueled party.

Ryan Quinney, who played in Reactionary 3 with Travis Fristoe and in Fiya, among other bands, was heavily involved with Wayward Council and The Ark. He says those scenes helped strike a balance with some of the male-centric party vibes elsewhere in town.

"I really feel like there was a long and very strong era where Wayward had a really mixed demographic," Quinney says. "A mix between gay and straight and male and female....I think the Wayward scene and The Ark scene were really not just complemented by, but almost dominated by women. Everybody did a good job of having this environment of inclusion."

Fiya performing at Wayward Council's ten-year anniversary celebration at the 1982 Bar in Gainesville. *Photograph by Matt Walker.*

With Matt Sweeting as the bridge, The Hardback Café had in a way spawned the drastically different Wayward Council. There was never a paid staff or management structure, but Wayward thrived for years with the ample supply of dedicated volunteers devoting time and energy to keep it going, even after some of its founders like Predny, Fitzpatrick and Barber began to focus their efforts elsewhere. Occasionally the store would fall a little short on rent, but a quickly booked benefit show would pull together enough funds for another month.

# 19.

# AGAINST ME! OPERATES OUTSIDE THE SYSTEM

In many ways, Gainesville had developed a punk scene that a band could step right into and thrive, even without the aid of The Hardback. Much of the groundwork had been laid by the end of the 1990s, and new bands could reap the fruits of that labor. There were venues to play at, plenty of like-minded people to mingle with and lots of experienced punk bands to learn from. Yet, in 1999, a new band called Against Me! was operating almost completely outside of the punk foundation in Gainesville.

Against Me! took on different forms in its early incarnations, with founder, singer and guitarist Laura Jane Grace the only constant member. She could be seen playing around town with her acoustic guitar, sometimes accompanied by a bass player or sometimes with a drummer banging on pickle buckets repurposed from the Wine and Cheese Gallery downtown. Every now and then, another guitarist would show up in the mix as well.

In the beginning, the band wasn't booking shows at Common Grounds or Market Street. They could mostly be found at the Civic Media Center (CMC), a tiny nonprofit alternative library located just west of Wayward Council at the time that supports grassroots activism. While most punk bands inherently have a political or antiauthoritarian component, few Gainesville bands had been as deeply entrenched in activist causes as Against Me! when they started out.

Laura Jane Grace moved from Naples, Italy, to Naples, Florida, when she was twelve years old. As a major in the U.S. Army, Grace's father was stationed in Italy, but when her parents divorced, Grace's mom moved Grace and her brother back to the United States to live with Grace's grandmother.

Grace, who was born Thomas James Gabel and came out as transgender in 2012, was into punk music from a young age. She and bassist Dustin Fridkin had been playing music together since the seventh grade, and they met drummer Kevin Mahon the following year and soon brought him into the mix. Then, on their first day of high school, Grace and Fridkin met future guitarist James Bowman after they spotted him walking through the hallway with a green Mohawk.

Grace and Fridkin played in bands through their teenage years, most notably The Adversaries. The band played occasionally around the Naples region at all-ages venues or record stores, and they would frequently play in Fridkin's parents' garage, where they would bring in crowds of around fifty people. The band even played at The Hardback in Gainesville. Like Pung years before, the place was nearly empty when they played—except for Danarchy.

The idea of what punk rock meant for Grace crystallized when she was beaten and arrested by police in Naples after they instructed her to move off of a busy boardwalk so as not to block the flow of traffic, which she did. Yet they grabbed her and slammed her head down on the police car as they searched her pockets, brutalized and eventually hogtied her. Grace was charged with battery on a law enforcement officer and resisting arrest with violence—at the age of fifteen.

Grace would write about it years later in a blog post:

> *The experience politicized me. I dropped out of high school. I started doing a 'zine. I started a distro of political pamphlets and anarcho-punk records. I started a Food Not Bombs chapter with a group of friends. We met other like-minded people across Florida and started a radical activist network. We organized protests, we organized gatherings, workshops, participated in direct action.*

That was where Against Me! were coming from. Although Grace was aware that Gainesville had a vibrant punk scene, when she moved to town, it was the activism that initially attracted her. Grace says Gainesville and the CMC were the center of the activist scene in Florida at the time.

"The intention of the band starting out was really to be a part of the protest movement, and there wasn't a lot of future planning when it came down to it," Grace says. "Living then, it was like, 'Ok, where are we going to dumpster dive at?' or 'I've got to sell my plasma on Tuesdays and Thursdays.'"

In a few short years, Grace had gone from being a fan of punk bands like Green Day and Rancid to being influenced by anarcho-punk pioneers like Crass, Poison Girls and Omega Tribe. When she started writing her own songs, she turned to the only guitar she owned, a beat-up old acoustic, which would form the basis of Against Me!'s early sound.

Grace self-released an Against Me! demo tape in 1997 and another demo, *Vivida Vis!*, on which she is accompanied by Kevin Mahon and his makeshift drums, in 1998. The following year, Grace booked Against Me!'s first month-long tour, using *Book Your Own Fuckin' Life*. She said on the podcast *Turned Out a Punk* that about ten of the shows actually happened and the rest of the time she and Mahon spent sleeping in rest stops and begging for food at fast-food restaurants. It was on that tour that they met Jordan Kleeman, who was running a small record label called Crasshole. Kleeman was impressed by the group and agreed to put out their next release, a twelve-inch EP. But, because of a mastering error, only a very small number of the records were released.

Against Me!'s first release that really began to gain traction in the underground punk and activist circles was 2001's *Crime as Forgiven by Against Me!* EP. It was also the first time Grace and Mahon worked with Rob McGregor in Gainesville. He recalled:

> *They showed up with this ratty acoustic guitar that could not be worth more than twenty dollars, and a bunch of buckets and pots and pans. I remember scratching my head and wondering how I was going to make this sound good. Make no mistake, I was excited, because I love something different and a challenge. I fell in love with those guys immediately, especially Laura. Their music was so joyous, rebellious, hopeful, angry, idealistic, poetic, whimsical and tough. I knew a few people would love it fervently like I did, but I had no idea they would go on to become such a huge influence. I adored every moment I spent with them, including their later incarnations.*

"More people bought [*Crime*] than I think anybody expected," Fridkin says. He had rejoined the group shortly after the EP was released. "The sets we played started getting more singalong-y. It was a fairly steady build from that point. We started playing around town more, people started noticing us more, our shows started getting bigger."

Sweeting says the band definitely operated outside of the usual punk circles in Gainesville in those days. "I thought it was pretty neat that they

Against Me! in 2002 in Portland, on tour with fellow Gainesville band Fiya. *Photograph by Ryan Quinney.*

made their own crowd. I had such respect for that because they did not tap into the crowd that was really happening in Gainesville at most punk shows."

Guitarist James Bowman was back with the group by that time, and Against Me! headed on the road for their first tour as a four-piece. The tour went well, but it ended in near-catastrophe on their way back to Gainesville. The band was driving south on Interstate 75 just north of Atlanta when they were rear-ended by a semi-truck. The van was totaled, but the band members made it out with only minor injuries.

"James busted out the passenger side window with his head," Fridkin says, "which I know for sure because he rode with me on the drive home—somebody drove my car up from Gainesville—and James was picking pieces of glass out of his scalp."

After the wreck, Mahon left the band for good. For the time being, only Grace and Fridkin carried on as Against Me!, recording a self-titled EP that would come to be known as *The Acoustic EP* later that year with McGregor. Bowman returned to the band shortly thereafter, and they recruited drummer Warren Oakes, a Gainesville native who grew up in Sarasota and whose path had crossed with Against Me! over the years.

It was around that time that Sweeting says he realized Against Me! might be "a thing."

"It was a Rumbleseat show, Rumbleseat and Rob McGregor, and since Rob had recorded them I think he invited them to play....Against Me! rolls up, and I swear to God they had like fifty of their friends with them," Sweeting says. "They walked in with this army of eighteen-year-old kids and they fucking took over and went bananas and they all left....I was like, 'Goddamn! That was crazy.'"

With their more solidified four-piece lineup in place, the band had gone back to the studio with McGregor to record their debut full-length, *Against Me! Is Reinventing Axl Rose*. Kleeman, who had moved to Gainesville by that time, paid for the recording but didn't have the means to press the record and release it. Through Against Me!'s seven-inches and tours, word was spreading quickly about them through the underground. They discussed the possibility of releasing *Reinventing* on Ebullition, but owner Kent McClard ultimately passed on it. They also had an offer from A-F Records, which was started by the like-minded activist punk band Anti-Flag.

"They wanted to sign us to this, like, six- or seven-album contract," Grace says. "It would have fucking killed the band."

Bowman says, "A binder of a contract showed up and I remember, I was living right down on Second Avenue, and we were all looking at it, and we were like, what the fuck? There's no way."

Eventually, Kleeman met with Var Thelin, whom none of the band members knew at that point, to see if No Idea would be interested in releasing the album. Thelin agreed to put it out, and *Reinventing Axl Rose* was released in the spring of 2002.

Many fans' first introduction to Against Me! was via *Reinventing Axl Rose*. Past incarnations of Against Me! had toyed with the elements that would ultimately come together on *Reinventing* in the perfect combination of raw authenticity, unstoppable energy, political and personal lyrics, unbridled enthusiasm and some of the most anthemic singalong punk choruses to come out of Gainesville.

But it was at Against Me!'s live shows that their passion and energy were fully realized. Their shows were hot and sweaty affairs, usually in venues filled beyond capacity with hundreds of voices singing along to the infectious choruses led by Grace and Bowman. The energy they gave off and got back from the crowd was beyond anything most bands ever achieve. As a four piece, Against Me! had hit its stride, and their reputation as one of the best punk bands in the country began to form.

By this time, the band had also integrated more fully into the Gainesville punk community. The members had become friends with some of the

Against Me! performing in 2004 at Bogart's in Cincinnati, on tour with Anti-Flag and Rise Against. *Photograph by Bryan Wynacht.*

Gainesville on tour: members of Against Me!, Army of Ponch and Grabass Charlestons in Atlanta in 2002. *Photograph by Heather Lacy.*

*Opposite, bottom*: Bitchin' performs in Gainesville. *Photograph by Todd Weissfeld.*

politically minded punks in the scene developing around the newly opened Wayward Council and were playing shows with No Idea bands.

"There was like that scene of bands in Gainesville, like Bitchin', Gunmoll, Army of Ponch, a couple of others that were really kind of happening," Grace says. "That was when it felt like we were really starting to be accepted by other bands in town and it felt like we were becoming part of the scene."

Things had been on a fairly slow but steady progression for Against Me! up until that point, but once *Reinventing Axl Rose* came out, things really began to take off. The group began their near-endless tour schedule, which would be a trend for years to come, sometimes staying on the road for eight or nine months out of the year.

# 20.

# GAINESVILLE PUNK FOR
# THE NEW MILLENNIUM

Against Me! was leading the charge for Gainesville punk in the early 2000s, but as always, there was a rich and vibrant punk scene in town. Another new wave of bands was forming that would help to define the scene, as it once again reinvented itself in the new millennium. The Hardback was dead; Wayward Council was in full swing; Common Grounds, Market Street and others were providing venues for the bands to play; and another generation was formulating its own blend of punk rock in various mixtures. And with punk rock approaching its third decade, there was a deep and diverse roster of influences from which to pull. And those new bands were touring—a lot.

After The Hardback came to an end, Drew DeMaio would go on to play in the melodic and atmospheric indie band Argentina and South Florida heavy rockers Floor. Matt Sweeting jumped right into a new project with former Palatka members Ryan Murphy and Mark Rodriguez and Dave Diem of Twelve Hour Turn. The band was called True North, and they immediately began recording and touring. The band's approach was a contrast for Murphy and Rodriguez, as they went from eschewing stages altogether to being included on some of the bigger tours in the underground, playing often with Blood Brothers and Against Me! and even opening for Fugazi in Gainesville.

True North used the most rhythmic and discordant elements of Washington, D.C.'s punk scene as a starting point and then put their own spin on it, bringing experimental and innovative hardcore into the new millennium. *Maximum Rocknroll* dubbed the band the "future of hardcore."

True North performing at the final night of Common Grounds' original location. *Photograph by Aaron Kahn.*

Samantha Jones was going full-force in Bitchin', which represented Gainesville throughout the United States and Europe with catchy, sometimes aggressive dual vocals and music that was a perfect balance of melodic post-hardcore and speedy old-school punk influences—all presented with an effortless sense of cool.

Brian Johnson of Section 8 and Assholeparade would go on to form Whiskey & Co., a classic-style country band that took a hard-partying and at times nihilistic punk rock mindset and laid it over twangy guitars and two-step rhythms.

Army of Ponch also sprang up during this period, and they proved to be one of the best bands in the country to mix post-hardcore and emo elements into a sound much more authentic than the watered-down "screamo" and mall punk that would soon dominate popular rock. Their live shows captured raw energy and emotion other bands could only imitate. Jack Bailey, who sang and played guitar in Ponch, had also played in the Blacktop Cadence with Chris Wollard and George Rebelo and in Baroque with Samantha Jones. Bailey says bands like Fugazi and Quicksand were early influences on Ponch, but they were really driven by all the cool music they saw their friends making.

Army of Ponch performing at the Atlantic in Gainesville. *Photograph by Marisol Amador.*

"It just became us trying to keep up with our peers," Bailey says. "We were influenced by the bands we were playing with—Twelve Hour Turn and Strikeforce Diablo—I wanted to write songs like that."

Fiya was playing smart and innovative hardcore with intricate musicianship and thoughtful lyrics wrapped in an aggressive but catchy package. The band developed in the house-show scene in the wake of The Hardback and would move on to playing frequently at Wayward Council and The Ark. They became friends with Against Me! early on. Brothers Ryan and Patrick Quinney from Fiya, along with Samantha Jones and Todd Weisfeld of Bitchin', were among the group who sang backup vocals on *Reinventing Axl Rose*.

Grabass Charlestons would become a near-constant presence in the Gainesville scene in the next decade, as well. The band started out as a loose and speedy pop-punk band on the gruffer side of the genre before evolving into a group putting out some of the most carefully crafted and thoughtful punk to come out of Gainesville.

Each of these bands would release albums on No Idea, in addition to various seven-inches and comp tracks on other labels, some based in Gainesville

Grabass Charlestons play at a house show. *Courtesy of Dave Drobach.*

(Obscurist Press, Barracuda Sound, Sabot) and some outside of Gainesville. With the exception of Bitchin', they would continue to play through the rest of the decade, each helping to define a portion of the Gainesville punk scene of the 2000s. Like the '90s, the Gainesville scene in the 2000s was awash in great bands. Others that could regularly be seen around town in the early part of the new millennium included The Belltones, Gunmoll, Towers of Hanoi, Hello Shitty People, Billy Reese Peters, Rehasher and Escape Grace.

# 21.

# AGAINST ME! RISES TO NATIONAL STAGE

In the summer of 2002, Against Me! and Fiya went on a month-long tour, which would be Fridkin's last with the band. Fridkin was always somewhat torn between playing in the band and going back to college to finish his education. He also wasn't a big fan of constant touring, so continuing his schooling ultimately won out. He told the band that the summer tour would be his last.

After parting ways amicably with Fridkin, Against Me! was on the hunt for a new bass player. The search didn't last long though.

Against Me! had played a couple of shows with a Murfreesboro, Tennessee band called Kill Devil Hills and had hit it off with their bass player, Andrew Seward. He and Grace exchanged emails. Seward and his bandmates were huge fans of the band and would listen to *Reinventing Axl Rose* frequently on the road. Seward said that, eventually, things started going south in Tennessee, and one night, he drunkenly and jokingly emailed Grace: "Hey, you should kick out your bass player and let me join the band."

"And I get an email response like that night or the next morning, it was very quick, saying, 'Are you serious? Because Dustin's going back to college, we actually need a bass player. If you move down here you can be in the band,'" Seward says.

Seward was in Gainesville within two weeks, with a bike, his bass and an amp, and he slept on Jordan Kleeman's floor for the first month before getting a garage apartment near Nigel Hamm from Common Grounds. Seward jumped right into things, recording the *The Disco Before*

Against Me! performing in the mid-2000s. *Photograph by Bryan Wynacht.*

*the Breakdown* seven-inch single with Against Me! within the first months of living in Gainesville.

As the hype around the band continued to grow, they were approached by Fat Wreck Chords, owned by Fat Mike of NOFX, to see if the band was interested in putting out an EP on the label. Since they had just released *The Disco Before the Breakdown*, Against Me! said they would rather release a full-length, to which the label agreed.

*Against Me! as the Eternal Cowboy* was released on Fat Wreck Chords in 2003, and everything was a steady rise as Against Me! continued to gain more and more fans. But as the band outgrew playing tiny punk houses and seemed to drift further from the activist circles it was born in, a vocal minority of former fans reacted loudly to Against Me!'s success. Against Me! had gotten flak every step of the way in its progression, from having their van's tires slashed to people forming protests outside their shows. As a testament to the way they treated people in their hometown scene, Against Me! detractors were few and far between in Gainesville, however.

"If I look back on it, I think we did nothing but grow in a completely natural way. I always think we kept it completely real," Seward says. "We knew where we came from. Just like everybody else, we were [practicing] in a sweatbox out on 74th. It's a fucking warehouse, you can't hear anything. I remember when we wrote *Cowboy* we'd be out there practicing, it's just so fucking loud....Then when you get in the studio it's like, 'Oh, you're playing that? I've never heard that before. I could never hear you at practice.'"

"Even after we released *New Wave* and *White Crosses*, stuff like that, we would play random house shows in Gainesville under the name Gift Certificate or the Bitchy Ponies or stuff like that," Seward says. "I still don't think the band has ever been too big for their britches."

In 2004, Jake Burghart filmed a documentary of Against Me! on the road with Planes Mistaken for Stars and No Choice. The documentary follows the band as they are being courted by various major record labels and shows how they navigate the awkward waters of being a punk band dealing with music industry executives. The band ultimately turned down the offers at the time but announced in 2006 that they were signing to Sire Records, for which they would record *New Wave* with legendary music producer Butch Vig, who recorded Nirvana's *Nevermind,* among many other classic albums.

*New Wave* would break into the mainstream, peaking at 57 on the Billboard charts. It was named the No. 9 best album of 2007 by *Rolling Stone* and was named Album of the Year by *Spin Magazine.*

# 22.

# THE VENUES
# SHUFFLE ONCE MORE

By 2004, Common Grounds had become a go-to spot for punk shows and was outgrowing the small space formerly dedicated to brewing coffee and providing a nice quiet atmosphere for a chess game. Co-owners Nigel Hamm and Naomi Nelson, along with Jason Rockhill, decided to partner together to reinvent Common Grounds as a full-on show venue in a new location. Rockhill says he had gotten tired of driving in circles around the country as Hot Water Music's tour manager and was interested in finding a more stationary career for a while. Common Grounds relocated to the old Covered Dish building and, after some remodeling, opened the doors to the punk scene once more. Common Grounds and its outside area, the Porch, attracted a regular crowd of Gainesville punks, and with a capacity of around four hundred people, it booked most of the mid- to large-sized punk shows in town. Common Grounds was not a replacement for The Hardback, nor was it meant to be, but it was where one could find Danarchy most nights and members of Hot Water Music occasionally working behind the bar between tours.

The same year, the Atlantic would replace the Down-Lo, near the corner of University Avenue and Main Street, right around the corner from where the Vatican once hosted some of Gainesville's early punk shows. The punk-friendly Atlantic would host many local punk shows as well as mid-size shows for touring punk bands.

Between Wayward Council, Common Grounds, the Atlantic and the new 1982 Bar (which took up residence in the old Common Grounds location),

Burnman performing at The Fireside Bowl in Chicago, on tour with 12 Hour Turn and True North. *Photograph by Matt Geiger.*

by 2004, Gainesville was flush with punk-friendly venues that would last at least to the end of the decade.

The Ark didn't make it quite as long. After the owners of the building saw an opportunity for more money, they decided not to renew the lease so they could attract higher bidders. In 2007, Gainesville punks said farewell to The Ark with four days of shows that included many of the active Gainesville punk and indie bands of the day, like Grabass Charlestons, Beat Buttons, Fiya, Reactionary 3, Laserhead, Towers of Hanoi, Stressface (a joke-y hardcore band composed of No Idea employees), Savage Brewtality, Apeshit, Young Livers and more. Having played the very first Ark show in 1999, the Marburger brothers with Darren Kucera also played a Burnman reunion set.

Against Me! even played on the second day; flyers advertised them under one of their silly aliases, "DJ Rastacakes," so as not to be flooded by fans from the community. Word was spread through the punk circles that DJ Rastacakes was actually Against Me! and anybody who wanted to see them should be there early. Their set was done before dark, and sure enough, college kids from UF who rarely ventured to the east side of town had somehow gotten wind of the show and were turning up to ask if they were in the right place to see Against Me!

# 23.

# THE FEST USHERS IN ANOTHER NEW ERA FOR GAINESVILLE PUNK

As the Gainesville punk scene's influence spread across the nation over the years, punk fans might have associated it at times with No Idea Records, Hot Water Music, Less Than Jake, Wayward Council, The Hardback or others, depending on the era and audience. But by the mid-2000s, The Fest would certainly be added to that list.

Tony Weinbender had left Fueled by Ramen in 2001 after butting heads too many times with John Janick. He felt like he was floundering in town and was looking for something productive to put his energy into.

"I had no plan, no backup plan. I started just kind of like being really broke for a while, donating plasma and selling off my musical collection," Weinbender said in a 2013 interview. "And then I ended up working and waiting tables at some restaurants. I moved furniture for a while. I just did whatever I could to get by."

A number of Weinbender's friends from Virginia had moved to town by then, and they were all drinking beer on someone's porch one day when the idea came up for Weinbender to plan a music festival in Gainesville, since he had been involved in organizing MACRoCk in Virginia. He took the idea and ran with it.

Weinbender went to work planning what was then a two-day festival, reaching out to bands he knew in Gainesville (and some he didn't know) and to the bands he had made connections with over the years in Virginia and through Fueled by Ramen. He borrowed $1,000 from each of his parents to help cover preliminary costs, like printing flyers and promotional materials and setting up a website.

Back in Virginia, Weinbender and his friends would call just about any opportunity to go out and drink or watch bands a "fest." The word was a synonym for any opportunity to party. So it seemed like a natural choice to simply call the new festival The Fest.

Weinbender says one of the biggest challenges early on was differentiating it from the earlier Gainesville Hardcore Fest of the late 1990s.

P.J. Fancher, who played guitar in Grabass Charlestons and would soon work for No Idea and help run subsequent Fests, said there was some skepticism at first from the punk community. "I remember the feeling around town was like, 'Yeah, I guess we're playing this thing, this Fest or whatever,'" Fancher says. "We really had no idea how it was going to be. We thought it was going to be a huge mess, but it turned out really well. He organized it really well."

Fest 1 took place over the weekend of May 24–25, 2002. About half of the sixty bands that played were either Gainesville punk bands or bands closely associated with Gainesville. The others weren't far removed from those same circles, though. Punks from in town and from across the country converged in downtown Gainesville, bouncing around between the venues and catching up with old friends and touring buddies.

The Fest, which Weinbender calls a family reunion, wasn't like other music festivals. Rather than being held in a big field or parking lot, it was held in the same venues that hosted punk shows throughout the year in Gainesville. It had a distinct community vibe; most of the bands and fans knew each other in some way. Fest registration was held inside the tiny Wayward Council, and places like Common Grounds and Market Street hosted the shows.

Weinbender received good feedback from the Gainesville punk community, regrouped and, in 2003, decided to plan Fest 2 for the weekend of the Georgia-Florida football game, which is typically held in late October or early November—a tradition that continues through to today. The longtime rivals play the annual game in Jacksonville, Florida, on "neutral ground." The result is that a big part of the Gainesville locals either head to Jacksonville or stay home to watch the game, including UF frat boys and other college kids who might not respond well to their downtown bars and clubs being overtaken by punks.

Weinbender received support for The Fest early on from No Idea Records, and within a couple of years, he would be working at No Idea full time.

The Fest grew quickly, expanding to three days and five venues by its third year; by its fifth year, the festival included around two hundred bands across nine venues. Fest started becoming a punk scene unto itself in many ways.

Fest after-shows proliferated; some years, there would be a full schedule of bands playing house shows after the Fest shows had ended for the night. Bands would book their tours with the timing of Fest in mind, and some people were even moving to town based solely on their experiences at Fest.

In 2016, The Fest is still going strong, with around four hundred bands and nine venues involved. But Weinbender has intentionally tried to keep it from getting too large for the city. In recent years, the tickets have been capped at 3,250, a much smaller number than most of the fests around the country. With The Fest still a very big part of the current Gainesville scene, in its fifteenth year, it's one of the most far-reaching and impactful developments in the scene's history.

Gainesville punk carried on as strong as ever throughout the decade. In the 2000s, Less Than Jake continued to tour hard, maintaining their success on the national level. Jessica Mills and Derron Nuhfer had left the band by then, and saxophonist Peter "JR" Wasilewski was brought into the mix (Nuhfer went on to play in other Gainesville bands like Gunmoll and Cutman). They moved from Capitol Records to large indie label Fat Wreck Chords, with which they released 2000's *Borders & Boundaries*. They moved back to a major

Young Livers performing at a house show in Gainesville. *Photograph by Lindsay Beaumont.*

label once again, releasing two albums on Sire Records before going back to their independent roots once more with their own label, Sleep It Off Records, in 2008. Their latest album, *See the Light*, was released on Fat Wreck Chords in 2013.

Hot Water Music had moved up to large indie label Epitaph Records in 2001, where they released *A Flight and a Crash*, *Caution* and 2004's *The New What's Next*. In 2006, the group broke up once more; Chuck Ragan focused on his solo acoustic career, and the remaining members of Hot Water Music formed The Draft with former Discount bassist Todd Rockhill. Hot Water Music again reunited in 2008, and they continue to play sporadically but have put their days of extended touring behind them. They released *Exister* on Rise Records in 2012.

In the later part of the decade and moving into the 2010s, Young Livers continued spreading the No Idea name as they toured the country and Europe with their energetic and melodic post-hardcore. Post Teens proved to be one of the most exciting live bands in Gainesville in years, with their full-on power-chord assault wrapped around quick and catchy vocals. Mauser helped lead a d-beat revival and inspired a new wave of raw punk bands in Gainesville that are thriving in the scene's underground today. The list—like Gainesville punk—goes on.

# AFTERWORD

**D**ave Rohm leans in to the microphone. "You're one up on me but you'll get it back, you're one up on me, you're gonna get it back." The packed crowd takes a collective breath before the chorus surges in, and nearly everybody in the room sings in unison, drowning out Rohm's microphone: "Bow down to me, bow down to me. Radon, radon, radon, radon!" The bodies press together, swaying back and forth; people point and scream and reach for the mic as giant, oversized cotton underwear fly through the air, landing on Rohm and crew. Just another Radon show at The Hardback—in 2016.

As this book was being written, Alan Bushnell, who has been working for years now as a public defender in the area, decided to reopen his old venue. It's in a different location, this time on University Avenue just west of downtown, but the intent is the same. Live, local, original music. Just a few of the acts that grew up at the old Hardback that have played there in the past few months include Radon, King Friday, Less Than Jake, Grinch and Clay Smith of Highway 66. They're still booking young, up-and-coming bands, as well.

But, as always, venues come and go. Common Grounds shut its doors in 2011, with Nigel Hamm and Jason Rockhill moving on to other projects in town. And Wayward Council closed in 2012. But Daniel Halal, a longtime Wayward volunteer, partnered with No Idea to open Arrow's Aim Records on North Main Street. In 2015, 1982 Bar closed after a couple of changes of ownership. But the Atlantic remains, and Loosey's is also a big supporter of the Gainesville punk scene.

There has also been a recent surge of super underground punk bands thriving at unofficial DIY venues and punk houses. Gainesville punk is reinventing itself once more.

The original Hardback location remains closely affiliated with the Gainesville punk scene. In 2009, drummer Warren Oakes parted ways with Against Me! and went into business with two friends, opening the Mexican restaurant Boca Fiesta in the building that was once The Hardback Café. Soon after, they opened The Backyard in the adjacent courtyard, which frequently hosts punk shows.

After more lineup changes, Against Me! is still thriving, releasing the acclaimed *Transgender Dysphoria Blues*, their sixth studio album, in 2014.

Assholeparade celebrated its twentieth anniversary in 2015 with two nights of shows at the Wooly in Gainesville, featuring guest sets from friends and tourmates over the years, including Radon as well as a Palatka reunion.

No Idea Records is also still going strong and just put out its 350th release, *No Anchor* by Chris Wollard's band, Ship Thieves.

Most of the musicians mentioned in this book are still in active bands or heavily involved in the music scene in some form today.

One last thing.

During the process of researching and writing this book, the Gainesville punk community (and many people far beyond) mourned the loss of Travis Fristoe, who was an important part of many people's lives. I met Travis around 2007, when we were both contributing to *The Satellite* magazine. I never got to know him beyond being friendly acquaintances, but over the years he showed me nothing but kindness, good humor and support when our paths crossed. I had been corresponding with him in late 2014 and early 2015 about this book. Again, he offered nothing but support and imparted some great advice and wisdom to someone with a fraction of the writing chops and musical knowledge he possessed. The last email he sent me was in March 2015, and we were commiserating about writing, friends and family. In closing, he wrote, "Here's to it, all of it." That sounded perfect to me. Here's to it, Travis. R.I.P.

# BIBLIOGRAPHY

Bayer, Jonah. "The Oral History of Hot Water Music." *Alternative Press*, November 2006, 126–32.

Blumel, Philip. "Nation Reads Local Students' 'fanzines.'" *Gainesville Sun*, December 9, 1988.

Blush, Steven, and George Petros. *American Hardcore: A Tribal History*. Los Angeles: Feral House, 2001.

Braunstein, Janet. "Traveling Musicians." *Independent Florida Alligator* (Gainesville), October 7, 1983.

Chadwick, Andrew. "Gainesville Hardcore Festival." *Ink 19*, February 4, 1998. Web. Accessed April 27, 2016.

Farris, Michael A. "Mutley Chix, Serving Up Punk." *Independent Florida Alligator* (Gainesville), April 12, 1985.

Fitzpatrick, Dan. "An Oral History in One Act." *Satellite*, April 2, 2008, 8–9.

Julin, Diane. "Life in a Rock Band: Coping with the Irritations." *Independent Florida Alligator* (Gainesville), September 16, 1981.

Maggio, J. "Against Me! Loud and Fast All the Time." *Satellite*, January 6, 2003, 7–25.

"No Idea Records." No Idea Records. Accessed April 28, 2016. http://www.noidearecords.com.

Nordlie, Tom. "Welcome to My Nightmare." *Independent Florida Alligator* (Gainesville), July 10, 1986.

Porche, John. "Garage Bands—The Few, the Proud, the Underground." *Independent Florida Alligator* (Gainesville), November 22, 1985.

Resh, Jon. *Amped: Notes from a Go-nowhere Punk Band*. Chicago: Viper Press, 2001.

Rozsa, Lori. "Never Mind the Blood...Here Comes the Roach Motel." *Independent Florida Alligator* (Gainesville), January 21, 1983.

Tabb, George. *Surfing Armageddon: Fishnets, Fascists and Body Fluids in Florida*. Brooklyn, NY: Soft Skull, 2006.

Taylor, Todd. "Against Me!" *Razorcake*, October/November 2005, 50–61.

———. *Born to Rock: Heavy Drinkers and Thinkers*. Los Angeles: Gorsky Press, 2004.

———. "Interview with No Idea: Celebrating Their 25th Birthday." *Razorcake.org*, November 16, 2010. Web. Accessed November 24, 2014.

Walker, Matt. "Hot Water Music Reunites." *Satellite*, January 9, 2008, 8–9.

## INTERVIEWS

Bailey, Jack, and Gui Amador. Telephone interview by author. April 21, 2016.

Baldwin, Nina. Telephone interview by author. November 24, 2014.

Brightman, Peter. Telephone interview by author. February 2, 2015.

Brownell, Randy. Telephone interview by author. May 15, 2015.

Bryson, Bill. Interview by author. February 6, 2015.

Burja, Kurt. Email interview by author. April 19, 2016.

Bushnell, Alan. Interview by author. December 13, 2014.

Cervera, Jorge. Telephone interview by author. December 12, 2014.

Doherty, Brian. Online interview by author. March 13, 2015.

Fancher, P.J. Interview by author. October 10, 2008.

Fetzer, Debra. Interview by author. November 9, 2014.

Frey, Cindy. Interview by author. January 16, 2015.

Fridkin, Dustin. Interview by author. February 19, 2015.

Fristoe, Travis. Interview by author. January 2, 2015.

Getz, Sid. Telephone interview by author. October 21, 2015.

Ginn, Travis. Email interview by author. April 22, 2016.

Grace, Laura Jane, James Bowman and Dustin Fridkin. Interview by author. February 14, 2015.

Halal, Daniel. Online interview by author. March 26, 2015.

Hamm, Nigel, and Jason Rockhill. Interview by author. June 11, 2011.

Haven, Shane. Online interview by author. April 17, 2016.

Hodapp, Jeff. Telephone interview by author. November 22, 2014.

Huegel, Scott. Telephone interview by author. March 23, 2015.

# BIBLIOGRAPHY

Hughes, Patrick. Interview by author. December 21, 2014.

———. Online interview by author. March 11, 2015.

Johnson, Travis. Telephone interview by author. April 16, 2016.

Jones, Samantha. Interview by author. April 9, 2015.

Kruger, Brian. Interview by author. November 16, 2014.

Lassen, Sharon (Beatty). Telephone interview by author. November 30, 2014.

Lay, Aaron. Telephone interview by author. April 16, 2016.

Marburger, Jim, and Jon Marburger. Interview by author. December 20, 2014.

McGregor, Rob. Email interview by author. April 19, 2016.

Moyal, Damien. Telephone interview by author. February 12, 2016.

Murphy, Ryan. Telephone interview by author. April 2, 2016.

Nordlie, Tom. Email interview by author. January 18, 2015.

———. Interview by author. December 29, 2014.

Pinion, Charles. Telephone interview by author. December 11, 2014.

Quinney, Ryan. Telephone interview by author. April 20, 2016.

Ragan, Chuck. Telephone interview by author. April 2, 2011.

Rebelo, George. Interview by author. February 6, 2015.

Resh, Jon. Telephone interview by author. November 20, 2015.

Rockhill, Todd. Telephone interview by author. April 22, 2016.

Rodriguez, Mark, and Jason Teisinger. Interview by author. January 12, 2015.

# BIBLIOGRAPHY

Rohm, Dave. Interview by author. December 14, 2014.

Rohm, Dave, Rob McGregor, and James C. Bassett. Interview by author. October 4, 2014.

Sakany, Lois. Telephone interview by author. November 28, 2014.

Schaub, Buddy. Interview by author. November 6, 2015.

Seward, Andrew. Telephone interview by author. April 27, 2016.

Simmons, Joseph. Telephone interview by author. March 1, 2016.

Sweeting, Matt. Interview by author. March 15, 2011.

————. Telephone interview by author. April 19, 2016.

Tabb, George. Telephone interview by author. January 11, 2015.

Taylor, Mike. Email interview by author. April 15, 2016.

Thelin, Var. Interview by author. December 30, 2014.

Vito, Jennifer. Telephone interview by author. April 19, 2016.

Weinbender, Tony. Interview by author. February 12, 2011.

————. Telephone interview by author. April 27, 2016.

Wilkinson, Victor. Interview by author. December 7, 2014.

Wilson, Brent. Telephone interview by author. December 19, 2014.

# INDEX

# INDEX

# INDEX

# INDEX

# ABOUT THE AUTHOR

Matt Walker, a lifelong music fan, was born and raised in Valdosta, Georgia, and earned his BA in English literature from Valdosta State University. In 2006, he moved to Gainesville, where he earned his MA in mass communication with a focus on journalism from the University of Florida. He has been playing guitar for more than twenty years and has been involved in numerous bands during that time. He has been involved in writing about music since the early 2000s, serving at times as a columnist, writer and editor for a number of publications. He was the founder of the Gainesville-focused music website Lead Us Down, which remained active from 2011 to 2014. He currently works as a communications specialist at the University of Florida.